Hakuin

SEARCH

Edited by

Jean Sulzberger

1817

Published in San Francisco by
HARPER & ROW, PUBLISHERS
New York, Hagerstown, San Francisco, London

FIRST EDITION

Designer: C. Linda Dingler

COVER: Color drawing by Roland Topor

LIBRARY OF CONGRESS CATALOG CARD NUMBER: 78-4430

ISBN: 0-06-067766-X   79 80 81 82 83 10 9 8 7 6 5 4 3 2 1

ISBN: 0-06-067765-1 pbk   79 80 81 82 83 10 9 8 7 6 5 4 3 2 1

Go—not knowing where; bring—not knowing what; the path is long, the way unknown; the hero knows not how to arrive there by himself.

Russian fairy tale

CONTENTS

TRIANGLE

CIRCLE

Acknowledgments

A particular debt is owed to Henri Tracol of Paris, who was the consultant for *Search*.

The editor thanks a company of friends, the contributors, for their articles and stories; and P.L. Travers, Douglas Auchincloss, John Loudon, Roger Lipsey, Mavis Riordan, Richard Murphy, and Carlotta Kerwin for wise counsel and criticisms.

Special thanks are owed to Jay Brennan and Katsuko Yamazaki in Tokyo for help in getting permissions and illustrations from Japan, and to Herbert Mason, who loaned Dino Cavallari's paintings of Gilgamesh.

The generosity of the late Stanley Nott and of Norman Franklin at Routledge & Kegan Paul made it possible for *Search* to reprint a sizable portion of *The Conference of the Birds,* with new illustrations by Rosemary Nott.

Sengai's picture of the universe as an interlocked circle, triangle and square, reproduced on page xiv, courtesy of the Idemitsu Art Gallery, Tokyo, has given *Search* its format: three sections—Square, Triangle, Circle—representing levels of the one search.

Editor's Note

Search presupposes a spiritual attitude in its readers, a feeling of nostalgia for something lost or forgotten. "There comes a time," Aldous Huxley wrote, "when one asks even of Shakespeare, even of Beethoven, is this all?"

Something hidden exists which man cannot find until he is drawn, by who knows what crossing of influences, to search for a source of ideas that could gradually free him from his crystallized forms of perception and bring real knowledge of who he is.

The way toward self-liberation, the way for man to free himself from the self that he merely imagines, begins in ordinary life, represented in the opening articles of this book by the section called "Square."

When the ordinary world is seen in a new way, it loses its fictitious value; it appears to be going nowhere, and the search "out there" becomes more interiorized, and finds another orientation. In the domain of the "Triangle," the searcher awakens to a new current of energy in himself which could transform his being and relate him to a larger life.

The progressive discovery of hidden passages from one level to another, until man reaches the place where time and space are transcended, the place where the axis of the universe becomes the axis of his own being, is evoked in two classical examples of search in the "Circle."

J.S.

Circle, Triangle and Square.

Introduction

Man is born a seeker.

Equipped as he is by nature for vibrating to a vast range of impressions, is he not predestined to an endless wondering? Bound by necessity to select from these impressions those suitable for conscious assimilation—and thereby to approach a genuine perception of his own identity—is he not singled out for continuous self-interrogation?

Such is his true vocation, his birthright. He may forget it, deny it, bury it in the depths of his unconscious being; he may go astray, misuse this hidden gift and increase his own alienation from reality; he may even try to convince himself that he has reached, once and for all, the shores of eternal Truth. No matter; this secret call is still alive, prompting him from within to try, and to try increasingly, to realize the significance of his presence here on earth. For he is here to awake, to remember and to search, again and still again.

Search for what? it could be asked. Surely there must be a definite aim, a purpose, a mark to be hit in due course. Have we not been warned only too often by modern scientists that "if you don't know *what* you are looking for, you will never know what you actually find"? According to their view, mathematical predictability must always prevail over the fertile challenge of uncertainty. And none of them will listen if you venture to remark that to "know" beforehand inevitably means that you will never "find" anything. Indeed there is no escape from the old bugbear of "whatness" unless we remember Scotus Erigena's dictum, "God does not know what He is, because He is not any 'what.' "

This cannot but remind me of my last meeting with an aging friend who was about to undertake what he sensed would be his last journey to sacred places and wise men of the East.

Bidding him good-bye, I said, "I hope you will find what you are seeking." He replied with a peaceful smile, "Since I am really searching for nothing, maybe I shall find it."

Introduction

Let us get rid at once of a possible misunderstanding and clearly state that no real knowledge can ever be attained by mere chance. There is such fascination in the shifting lure of existence that it draws our interest away from the immediate perception of the essential. Letting oneself drift into persuasive "visions" and "discoveries," no matter how seductive, or yielding to the spell of what could be called "search for the sake of searching," is merely to indulge in daydreaming—a form of self-tyranny very much at variance with man's objective needs.

Then how is one to set about an authentic quest? Instead of surrendering at once to the call of any particular "way," one should first try with humility to discern some of the requisites for setting off on the right foot.

Is not the first essential an act of *recognition*—recognition of the utter necessity of search itself, its priority, its urgency for him who aspires to awake and assume as fully as possible his inner and outer existence?

Whenever a man awakes, he awakes from the false assumption that he has always been awake, and therefore the master of his thoughts, feelings and actions. In that moment, he realizes—and this is the shadow side of recognition—how deeply ignorant he is of himself, how narrowly dependent on the web of relationships by which he exists, how helplessly at the mercy of any suggestion that happens to act upon him at a given moment.

He may also awake—if only for a flash—to the light of a higher consciousness, which will grant him a glimpse of the world of hidden potentialities to which he essentially belongs, help him transcend his own limitations, and open the way to inner transformation.

At such a moment the call to search resounds in him and hope is born in his heart. But woe betide him if he believes himself safe from now on. The vision does not last—perhaps it is not meant to last—and once more he is left with the dizzying impression of having sunk back into his own insoluble contradictions.

Feeling lost, he may lose himself further in his search for self-recovery; experiencing his blindness, he may increase it in trying to see; becoming aware of his slavery, he may let his very search for freedom fetter him still more.

Until suddenly he awakes anew, and the whole process begins again.

Introduction

In the long run, by trying and failing, over and over, he may come at last to attune himself to the specific part he has to perform in this enigmatic play.

Whenever a man awakes and remembers his purpose, he awakes to a fleeting miracle, and at the same time to an unanswerable riddle. He realizes, at moments, that in order for him to awake he was foredoomed to sleep; in order for him to remember, he was foredoomed to forget. Such is the law of this equivocal situation: without sleep, no awakening; without oblivion, no remembering. Hence, if he goes on looking for what is beyond ambivalence, it will prove to be merely another phantasm. In fact, there is, and always has been, a secret continuity in his being, which is partly reflected in the unchanging structure of his body and the regularly recurring activities of its functions. But in a perpetually moving world of energies, such a relative continuity can never be equated with immutability. The law of man's existence is to become—or to die. If a man were to stay still forever and merge into eternity, there would be little sense in his remaining here on earth.

Such is the human condition: a lucid and total acceptance of it is imperative. This alone will help the true searcher to reaffirm his inner determination. He must be ready to comply with a constantly shifting reality, ready to reconcile himself to the law of alternation, the law of successive turns of fate, ready to conform to whatever may be offered, either favorable or hostile, ready to reject all wishful thinking and to expect nothing in the way of result or reward.

Sooner or later, he will have to try not only to accept risks, but to take up the challenge *knowingly* and put himself in jeopardy. Only then will he truly respond to the call. Far from abjuring the revelations accorded him through teachings he may previously have come in contact with, he longs to "verify" them—that is, to prove them true for himself here and now. Conscious participation in what is self-evident is the goal of the genuine searcher: a goal so close and at the same time so remote, a goal so constantly offered and again withheld—in order that he may keep on searching.

For a man, far beyond his personal hopes and predilections, to search is a sacred task, and if he assents to it and persistently endeavors to fulfill it, he will experience it as truly corresponding both to his essential needs and to his specific capacities.

Introduction

Patience—much patience, endurance and determination, watchfulness and readiness, availability and conscious flexibility—all these are indispensable to the seeker.

Maybe the time will come when he realizes that in order to develop these latent potentialities he needs guidance and support. Freed from any pretension to be a "knower," he will deliberately put himself under the authority of a master. To absorb his teachings and follow his directives? Yes, and even more important, to perceive and to study the way he deals with life and people, to watch how he conveys his understanding through behavior and tone of voice, and, ultimately, to be able to receive his wordless glance.

By serving such an apprenticeship the seeker gradually unbinds himself from prejudice and becomes sensitive to a wide range of manifestations or testimonies of search, wherever he may happen upon them —and this regardless of any apparent inconsistencies he encounters between their respective features. He will realize that they all refer to the same Unknown that he himself confronts.

With this in mind, one may ask oneself why Sengai's eloquent drawing has been chosen as the motif for this book. Does not this Zen picture appear as a concluding gesture to what must have been, for the artist, a lifelong search? We cannot help visualizing Sengai preparing himself—hours of meditation in perfect stillness—then the smooth and careful stirring of the ink, and the brush rises, remains for a moment suspended in the air like an eagle watching its prey, until, all of a sudden —lo—it is done!

Circle, triangle, square.

But what kind of a geometrician is this man? Look at his "square"! The inaccuracy of the lines, the faintness of the ink! But Sengai, obviously, does not care: ordinary exactitude is no part of his province. Clearly, he is more concerned with the inner relationship among the three symbols and the way they engender one another.

Their sequence in itself is a riddle. If we ponder upon it, we realize that it naturally flows from right to left. Following the movement of the brush, we complete the circle, leave it for the triangle, and finally vanish into the last stroke of the square.

For us, it may be difficult to accept this interpretation of the sequence, since according to our Western system of associations, we automatically see it moving from left to right. That is the way we are trained to "read" things, reaching always toward the full stop and the closing of the circle.

There exist, in fact, reliable hints as to Sengai's probable intention. Professor D. T. Suzuki, the noted authority on Zen Buddhism, has suggested that the *circle* represents formlessness, emptiness or the void where there is yet no separation of light and darkness; the *triangle* evokes the birth of form out of formlessness; and the *square,* as a combination of two opposite triangles, stands for the multiplicity of things.

From the infinite oneness down to the inexhaustible variety of forms in which it divides itself, from the secrecy of Essence to the ever-springing Manifestation, here lies the mystery of involutive Creation.

But should we rest satisfied with Suzuki's marvelously condensed vision as the only reliable one? Or would such an easy consent not, in a sense, betray both painting and comment? Rather, we should keep our minds open to the flow of suggestions that comes from other sources, for instance the "squaring of the circle" of the Alchemists—and even those that may arise from our own inner recesses—while making sure that we do not fall under the spell of any of them.

Are we now ready to transcend the dangerous fascination of apparent contradictions?

Let us ponder the order given to the three sections of *Search* and the way it has been designed to tally with the left-to-right pattern. Here again, we are faced with the law of alternation, for now is the time to climb back to the source. Having been exiled to this small, remote planet, where our only possible chance of survival requires the protective ramparts of material stability *(square),* we have to find our way laboriously to the discovery of direction, guidance and consistency *(triangle)* until we are ready for the ultimate quest—the return to the origin, the beginning *(circle),* from where . . . but that is another story, or rather, perhaps the same story, the one everlasting story.

For the born searcher there is no escape from the labyrinth. Perhaps he will even realize that he himself is the labyrinth, and that no failure, no "answer" offered along the way, will ever stop him from moving further toward the center of his own mystery. And, far from trying to evade the challenge, he will hope to become more and more able to meet it: this alone will confer meaning upon his search.

Henri Tracol

xix

Now the real treasure, to end our misery and trials, is never far away; it is not to be sought in any distant region; it lies buried in the innermost recess of our own home, that is to say, our own being.. . . . But there is the odd and persistent fact that it is only after a faithful journey to a distant region, a foreign country, a strange land, that the meaning of the inner voice that is to guide our quest can be revealed to us.

Heinrich Zimmer

One day Nasreddin Khoja was chopping wood close to the road a few kilometers from Akshehir. After a while a man came along the road, walking toward Akshehir, and he called to Khoja, "Can you tell me how long it will take me to get to Akshehir?"

Khoja heard him and looked up from his work, but he said nothing. So the man called again, louder, "How long will it take me to get to Akshehir?"

Still Khoja said nothing, and this time the man roared like a lion, "How long will it take me to get to Akshehir?"

When Khoja did not answer even then, the man decided he must be deaf, and so he started walking rapidly toward the city. Nasreddin Khoja watched him for a moment, and then he shouted, "It will take you about an hour!"

"Well, why didn't you say so before?" demanded the man angrily.

"First I had to know how fast you were going to walk," answered the Khoja.

A Turkish tale

We none of us know where this stream comes from. As we have nothing to do this morning, wouldn't it be fun to follow it up to its source?

Wu Chʻêng-ên, Monkey

TWO TALES
BY MARTIN BUBER

I. The Treasure

Rabbi Bunam used to tell young men who came to him for the first time the story of Rabbi Eisik, son of Rabbi Yekel in Cracow. After many years of great poverty which had never shaken his faith in God, he dreamed someone bade him look for a treasure in Prague, under the bridge which leads to the King's palace. When the dream recurred a third time, Rabbi Eisik prepared for the journey and set out for Prague. But the bridge was guarded day and night and he did not dare to start digging. Nevertheless he went to the bridge every morning and kept walking around it until evening.

Finally the captain of the guards, who had been watching him, asked in a kindly way whether he was looking for something or waiting for somebody. Rabbi Eisik told him of the dream which had brought him here from a faraway country. The captain laughed: "And so to please the dream, you poor fellow wore out your shoes to come here! As for having faith in dreams, if I had had it, I should have had to get going when a dream once told me to go to Cracow and dig for treasure under the stove in the room of a Jew—Eisik, son of Yekel, that was the name! Eisik, son of Yekel! I can just imagine what it would be like, how I should have to try every house over there, where one half of the Jews are named Eisik, and the other half Yekel!" And he laughed again. Rabbi Eisik bowed, traveled home, dug up the treasure from under the stove, and built the House of Prayer which is called "Reb Eisik's Shul."

"Take this story to heart," Rabbi Bunam used to add, "and make what it says your own: there is something you cannot find anywhere in the world, not even at the zaddik's, and there is, nevertheless, a place where you can find it."

3

II. A Vain Search

Rabbi Hanokh told this story:

There was once a man who was very stupid. When he got up in the morning it was so hard for him to find his clothes that at night he almost hesitated to go to bed for thinking of the trouble he would have on waking. One evening he finally made a great effort, took paper and pencil, and as he undressed noted down exactly where he put everything he had on. The next morning, very well pleased with himself, he took the slip of paper in his hand and read: "cap"—there it was, he set it on his head; "pants"—there they lay, he got into them; and so it went until he was fully dressed.

"That's all very well, but now where am I myself?" he asked in great consternation. "Where in the world am I?" He looked and looked, but it was a vain search; he could not find himself. "And that is how it is with us," said the rabbi.

THE LOST CAMEL

Joseph Cary

You have lost a camel and the caravan is ready to depart. Your baggage lies scattered on the ground while you, pale with dismay, run through what is left of the encampment begging for clues, offering a reward. And the chance of quick profit produces a hundred improvised responses: yes, a reddish camel was headed toward the pasture; no, it was crop-eared and browsing by the spring; no, it had only one eye and an embroidered saddlecloth; yes, it was suffering from mange and passed this way not five minutes ago . . . But you, who know your camel even though you do not know where it is, know that such clues are false.

I paraphrase this story of a search from a translation of the *Mathna-wī* by the thirteenth-century Persian poet Rūmī. The seeker in the poem knows precisely what he has lost and so is able, even in a state of near despair, to distinguish correctly between good and bad advice. His story ends happily: he eventually encounters one whose description tallies with his knowledge, follows that man, and finds his camel.

But the poem contains another major figure, one more ambitious than the givers of false clues in that he covets the camel itself rather than the mere reward. His strategy is simple: he will *play* at having lost the lost camel and so gain at least a partner's share in it when it is found. He therefore mimics the true seeker's every word and gesture—the discovery of loss, the cries and tearing of hair, the wild rush through the camp and the pleas, the offering of reward. Taking his cue from the passionate sincerity in front of him, the false seeker apes discrimination, rejects what is rejected, turns and seems to try again, accepts at length what is apparently acceptable. His heart beats faster. There, wandering in the desert ahead, is the lost camel.

The story of the false seeker ends with his transformation. "When a liar sets out with a truthful man, his falsehood suddenly turns to truth." The impostor learns that the case he has been mimicking for gain is in fact his very own. In acting out the gestures of authentic loss and

5

search he is enabled to recall what his covetousness had hitherto concealed from him. He too has lost a camel. He ends by becoming a true seeker.

A scholarly note to the *Mathnawī* suggests that Rūmī's poem derives from a saying attributed to the prophet Mohammed: "Wisdom is the believer's stray camel." But for me what is most moving in the poem is what it says to the nonbeliever, to him who gives no credence to his search. The poem itself closes with a cautionary, almost rueful, word from the poet: "The subject of my discourse is not two camels; it is a single camel. Verbal expression is confined, the meaning to be expressed is very full." However I may choose to interpret this, it is clear at least that Rūmī himself has misgivings as to his expressive means (his words) and their adequate relation to his "meaning." He means more than he has been able to say, and he warns me to be on my guard.

And as for me, I trust neither the prophet Mohammed nor the poet Rūmī, but the poem before my eyes. It may be, as the citation from the Koran suggests, that I should understand "wisdom" where I read "camel." But will I ever feel for wisdom what I feel for my camel, that beast of burden I have tended and cursed and counted on and worked with and lived by all these years? It may be, as Rūmī says, that in the long run all camels—whatever their meaning—are one. But his poem says another thing: my camel is not yours. How should I not know my camel by heart? How could I be fooled by false clues? Wandering in the desert ahead, I shall know my camel when I find it. Already I think I recognize my brother—he who gives no credence to his search—and then my heart beats faster. I almost believe in my loss.

The poem says, "you have lost a camel," and sets my search where it must begin, here beneath my feet on the ground where my baggage lies scattered and the caravan is ready to depart. It is not truth or wisdom that I know so well, that I shall seek so passionately. It is not for the sake of truth or wisdom that I mime so expertly knowledge and passion. I swear I can live today and tomorrow without truth or wisdom, as I have in the past. But without my camel I am a ruined man.

"Trust in God, but tie your camel." Persian proverb.

6

SEARCHING HOME

Roger Lipsey

It is already late, by a child's standards; she is tucked in bed like her own doll, and she expects a story. I hunt among the books of tales—Andrew Lang, the Brothers Grimm, Afanas'ev's Russian, an Ethiopian miscellany—and with her help pick a Navaho Indian collection devoted to Coyote, an appealing trickster who thrives in a rather violent prairie. I stretch out beside her and we begin; she stirs occasionally while listening, plays with the edge of the blanket or follows with her eyes a fly exercising in the room, but I know from previous experience that she is listening with the attention of a hunter. I don't really know what she is listening for, and never have, but I know that stories are serious for her and, differently no doubt, serious for me. I try to read well, little by little noticing that the strain and fatigue of the day leave my voice so that the story can ring, which is what it wants: it seems to seek a good speaker and can transform a parent into a bard. I rediscover a curious impression of serving the story, of acting as a vehicle for it on its way to her and to myself—for I acknowledge that as the story progresses I become fascinated, and the question could be raised: for whom exactly am I reading? The tale this evening narrates Coyote's approach to Bear-woman; he wants to marry her, but she discouragingly proposes that she'll have to kill him four times before he'll be a suitable husband. Coyote is resourceful and generally solves his problems by special, freshly invented methods. In this case, he decides to hide his heart in his tail; when she kills him, this precaution will permit him to jump up as alive as before. "Go ahead," he says, "start killing me."

We read on and reach dire turns of events: Coyote, greedy and unwise, arouses the jealousy of a band of spiders over the excellent match he has made, and they murder him before he has a chance to make the usual arrangements for his reappearance; Bear-woman, an-

7

gered and unjustly blaming her brothers, meets her death in a battle with them. Coyote's marriage lasts less than a week—and the ending would be hard to accept if we didn't know that in the last resort he is immortal: death for him is just a way of freshening up between stories.

I turn off the room light and turn on the night light, wish her good night, and she turns to the large world of sleep while I descend the narrow staircase to another part of the house. And I pause—for that story, that little entertainment intended only to round off her day and lead her inside where a night's sleep begins, has affected me, and now I have time to examine its effect. In the sediment of my impressions, something at the moment hard to identify has been stirred: an old remorse half-forgotten, an old hope—it appears to be both. Coyote's ruse is the clue; I wait for clarification. Gradually thoughts form that translate feelings into language, and I begin to experience the well-being associated with a real inquiry, really underway.

All of the times that I failed to take a secret action have come back to me! Like Coyote, I didn't avoid combat, but unlike him I rushed in often with my heart on my sleeve, reserving nothing, brandishing everything. I nearly asked to be killed, so poorly monitored was the act, and in that was a certain lack of self-respect, which leaves a trace.

Then again, it was his heart that Coyote hid; in this I sense another clue.

At such times of investigation, many things come together into a pattern that normally seem alien to each other. My eyes are distracted for a moment by the bird-feeder that we set out for winter: I recall how flocks of grosbeaks and redpolls gather during the daylight hours, scratching in the snow at a promising place for dropped seeds. It occurs to me that they are in the image of my thoughts, to which I return.

That Coyote hid his heart leaves me questioning: I never altogether believed the "heart" to be just a physical organ, nor just the seat of emotion. It has come to signify a deeper intelligence that doesn't operate with words but harbors a vivid awareness of people and events. Did Coyote protect *that* heart from violent encounters?

I know what is stirring in me now, and I even know for the moment what I mean by "knowing": the thought is clearly set in words, and beneath it the feelings roused by the tale are still alive.

I hear a vow whispering in me to remember more often, to hide my

heart in my tail when the occasion calls for it. The formulation is so cheerful that I smile.

That smile ends the pause. She must be asleep by now, and I will turn to other things. But I have a suspicion that nothing further this evening will seem quite so important in comparison.

(Author's note: The book read that evening is *Coyote Stories of the Navaho People*, ed. Robert A. Roessel, Jr., and Dillon Platero, published under the auspices of the Navaho Curriculum Center, Rough Rock Demonstration School, Rough Rock, Arizona, 1968.)

SEARCHING FOR SHAMBHALA

James George

> We all sense simultaneously a strong perfume.
> From where does it come, for we are surrounded
> by rocks? The lama whispers: "Do you feel the
> fragrance of Shambhala?"
>
> Nicholas Roerich

When I first went to the East eighteen years ago, I began to hear about Shambhala. The idea intrigued me. It evoked childhood memories of James Hilton's *Lost Horizon* and other stories of Shangri-la. But more than that, it tapped a longing in me—a quest, as I can see now, for a lost spiritual center. Slowly I began gathering bits of information and catching snatches of rumor, never dreaming of mentioning this to any but my closest friends. How strange that looking for a center should be considered so eccentric! I even wondered about it myself. Still the lure persisted, and the inner longing became also an outer search.

Today, the search for the center, for teachers and teachings, is all around us. In fact, the noisy pursuit of spiritual fads threatens to obscure the true search. But this more open atmosphere invites me to share the adventure of my search for the meaning of Shambhala.

What, then, is Shambhala? It is a complex idea, a myth, an image, but is it also a place, a center that exists on earth? It has been called the navel of our world, the link with the world of the sacred. It is traditionally located in the part of Central Asia where Tibetan Buddhism flourished, yet it is said to relate to all the traditions that stem from the Truth

11

as a hub to the spokes of a wheel. In every age there have been teachings, schools, traditions, churches to guide men in the search for Truth; the idea of Shambhala stands for that which is behind and above every authentic school, teaching and tradition. As such, it is the spiritual home of us all.

The Tibetan tradition speaks of Shambhala as a mystical kingdom or sanctuary sheltered behind high mountains. There the most esoteric traditions are preserved while spiritual values are eroded or disappear in the world outside. According to Tibetan texts, the hidden way to this sanctuary is so long and arduous, so guarded by natural and supernatural obstacles, that it is ultimately accessible only to those rare searchers who, purified in mind and heart, are single-minded in their aim. Anyone who has visited Buddhist monasteries of Central Asia will have heard of such searchers—holy men who, after a lifetime of discipline and meditation, disappear into the mountain wastes never to return.

In the *Shambhala lam-yig (The Way to Shambhala),* a rare eighteenth-century Tibetan book, translated into German by Albert Grünwedel in 1915, the third Panchen Lama writes that the realm of Shambhala is situated in a mountain region sheltered on every side by mighty snow ranges. The people who live there comprise a community of guardians of mankind who, it is said, are the source of the hidden knowledge of every authentic teaching in the world. Throughout history, they have sent emissaries into our world, and it is Shambhala that will rescue the world from chaos in its darkest last days.

The question whether such a mythical place actually exists somewhere on this planet gives rise to more immediate questions and tangible quests. Nicholas Roerich, the Russian scientist, explorer and painter, was persuaded, from the time of his famous expeditions through Central Asia (1925–30), that only in just such a community of guardians could there arise the consciousness of a New Age. Roerich came to believe that Lhasa, the capital of Tibet, was connected to a living Shambhala community, possibly by a network of underground tunnels. It was a belief apparently shared by Tibetan lamas with whom he talked. But other Tibetans have told me that Shambhala is not a place at all but a state of consciousness. And so the question arises whether there exists a state of consciousness that is the source and goal of all religious traditions, accessible to determined pioneers of the spirit. Obviously, with the increasing influence of the East on the West (as well as the recovery of some esoteric traditions in the West itself), this state of being has become not only a credible idea, but a focal concern of many lives.

I have never had the opportunity to penetrate Tibet directly, for my wife and I arrived in South Asia just after Tibet was sealed off by the Chinese Communists. However, over the past eighteen years we have spent many of our holidays in the magnificent mountains of South Asia that border Tibet. We were there simply to walk, photograph, explore and enjoy the land and its peoples, but we kept open and alert to any signs of an existing Shambhala, or something akin to it.

Some Tibetan friends believe that there are secret places tucked away in the mountains of eastern Bhutan and the North East Frontier Area of India, north of Assam on the Tibetan frontier. One of them even showed us a stone, about two feet by four, blocking a cave entrance to what he believed was a tunnel leading to just such a hidden valley, where those who have attained a sufficient degree of self-realization may merit the privilege of entering. These secret places are regarded not only as power centers of knowledge but also as places of refuge from disasters that have overwhelmed Tibet and may spread to other areas in our lifetime. They resemble Shambhala, however, in that such *bayeus*, as Tibetans call them, will preserve the knowledge of the Buddha's most secret Tantric teachings.

In Nepal we also visited places of great spiritual power, and met people who have been north of Kathmandu to Dolpo on the Tibetan border. There, in the valley of Mu Gompa (altitude: 12,000 feet), there is a meditation cave of the famous Tibetan teacher Milarepa. We ourselves have sat in a meditation circle of rocks said to have been used by the Indian sage Padmasambhava, who brought Buddhism to Tibet in the eighth century. A little off the mountaineers' route to the base camp of Mt. Everest and about a day's walk to the south, it lies on a saddle of high ground at about 16,500 feet, overlooking a green lake mirroring

10,000 feet of the most extraordinary vertical rock formations I have ever seen.

Twice, in particular, my wife and I found ourselves on the threshold of areas where the tradition of Shambhala is very much alive. Once we were in the hills of Darjeeling (northeast India), and at another time in Ladakh, near the boundary claimed by China. Both places are on the old trade routes between India and Tibet, and in both there are huge statues of the Maitreya Buddha, who as the messianic Buddha of the future is associated with Shambhala. The Maitreya statue in Ghom Monastery, on the edge of Darjeeling, is said to contain secret prophecies related to Shambhala, and there are paintings *(thankas)* depicting its protective circle of snow peaks.

Throughout the mountains of the great Himalayas north of the Indian subcontinent, there are scores of valleys and high places of extraordinary beauty and power. Bhutan, Sikkim, Darjeeling, Almora, Solo-kumbu, Kathmandu, Mustang, Kulu, Kashmir, Ladakh, Swat— these places are as magical and hedged about with mystery as their names. Central Asia is full of mountain-ringed oases which make tales of Shambhala not only credible, but almost tangible.

Ironically, I feel that I came closest to encountering Shambhala while sitting in the study of Canada House in New Delhi one evening in 1968. We had as our guest the well-known Tibetan teacher Chögyam Trungpa Rinpoche, who has since established himself as a teacher in the United States, and we asked him what he thought of the tradition of Shambhala. To our astonishment, he replied very quietly that, although he had never been there, he believed in its existence and could see it in his mirror when he went into a certain state. He could reach this state by the traditional process of *prasena,* or "conjuration," through performing a special ritual invocation *(sādhana).* That evening in our study he produced a small metal mirror of the Chinese type. After looking intently into it for some time, he began to describe what he saw. Within a vast circle of high snow-capped mountains lay a green valley and a beautiful city, in the center of which rose a terraced hill with a small palace or temple on top of it. Around this hill was a square, walled enclosure, and around this again were other enclosures containing temples, gardens and sacred monuments. The most singular thing about the inhabitants of the city was that they were of all faiths, races and nations and appeared to come from the four corners of the earth.

Four years later, in Bhutan, I saw for myself the scene that Trungpa had described. It was in a painting that resembled in almost every detail the city that he had seen in his mirror. I saw it at the home of one of the senior officials and nobles of Paro, Mr. Paljor Dorji. Mr. Dorji confirmed that his painting, which was several centuries old, was of Shambhala. And it also compared well with a Tibetan map of Shambhala which a Bōn priest had given to me in India, though the Tibetan version is considerably more stylized.

The questions that we ask today about Shambhala have, of course, been posed by others before us, for the concept of a hidden spiritual kingdom and all it implies has always had an irresistible appeal. My subsequent conversations, reading and research broadened and deepened my encounters with the central core of the Shambhala tradition. So far as we know, the first Europeans to write of it were two Portuguese Jesuits, Estevão Cacella and João Cabral. Although these missionaries made few converts in Bhutan, they won the confidence of the Tibetan Buddhists there to such an extent that they were invited to go to Shambhala in 1627, when they were seeking the route to Cathay. Their search took them to Tibet but not to Shambhala; Cacella died in 1650 in Shigatse, still yearning for a glimpse of the "magical country" that lives in the pages of his travel letters.

Given his interest in the occult and in divine revelation, it is not surprising that the Swedish scientist, philosopher and theologian, Emanuel Swedenborg, should have become fascinated by the concept of Shambhala and written about it in the eighteenth century. Swedenborg's references to Shambhala went largely unremarked, however, and it remained for the Russian Theosophist Madame Helena Blavatsky to give the idea wider currency in the nineteenth century, when she placed the sacred city in the Gobi Desert.

Since then the Shambhala idea has touched such diverse thinkers as Nicholas Roerich, Ferdinand Ossendowski, Mircea Eliade, René Guénon, René Daumal, Alexandra David-Neel, Giuseppe Tucci, and G. I. Gurdjieff. In one form or another they have each asked the question: Does there exist a hidden community of men who actually live at the

Kingdom of Shambhala.
An oasis encircled by snow-capped mountains.

Map of Shambhala.
The Nine-Stage Swastika Mountain.

heart of tradition, finding and handing on the primordial wisdom that sustains all authentic religious teaching? René Daumal, for instance, in his unfinished novel, *Mount Analogue,* has his hero, Sogol, say:

"I had heard about a superior type of man, possessing the keys to everything which is a mystery to us. This idea of a higher and unknown strain within the human race was not something I could take simply as an allegory. Experience has proved, I told myself, that a man cannot reach truth directly, nor all by himself. An intermediary has to be present, a force still human in certain respects, yet transcending humanity in others. Somewhere on our Earth this superior form of humanity must exist, and not utterly out of reach. In that case shouldn't all my efforts be directed toward discovering it?"

Daumal's novel is about the way to a hidden island, unmapped by human exploration, out of which rises a Cosmic Mountain to be climbed. Although I have no way of knowing what his Sanskrit sources were, he was probably familiar with accounts of the travels of Buddha Gupta, a sixteenth-century Indian Buddhist and yogi, who traveled widely from Madagascar to Indonesia. In his *Guide Book to Potala Mountain Journey,* he records finding an island with a huge crystal mountain which was invisible to most people at most times because of the quality of the light emanating from it. Buddha Gupta saw it one evening, but did not manage to land on the island.

The quest for a sacred community, inaccessible to ordinary human approaches, is of great antiquity. The Chinese historian, Ssu-ma Ch'ien (163–85 B.C.), says that in the times of the ancient kings, "men began to be sent to sea to search for the three holy mountains which are said to be not far away from men; unfortunately, when one has almost reached them, the boat is carried backward by the wind and driven off course. Formerly, it is said, people were able to get there; there dwell the Blessed, and there is kept the drug of immortality; there, all beings, birds and quadrupeds are white, and the palaces are made of gold and silver. Before arriving, people saw them from afar like clouds; when they got there, the three holy mountains were found upside down under the water . . . In a word, no one has been able to reach them, though there has never been a leader of men who has not desired to go there."*

*Quoted by Max Kaltenmark in *Lao Tseu et le Taoïsme,* Editions du Seuil, Paris, 1965, p. 149.

Records as far back as the third and second centuries B.C. show that
Chinese emperors sent expeditions charged with seeking the Palace of
Immortals hidden in the K'un-Lun mountains of northern Tibet. The
Taoists have long believed in a lost mountain country of Tebou, whose
inhabitants live permanently and simultaneously in two worlds—a ma-
terial and spiritual one. Lao-Tzu (born ca. 604 B.C.) is said to have left
China at the end of his life and journeyed to the Land of the Immortals.
He is often depicted on the back of a water buffalo heading to the
legendary land of the West.

The ancient search continues today. A few months ago, I had the
opportunity of talking to Pema Wangyal, the Taklung Tsetrul Rin-
poche, about his journey in 1954 with his late father, the Ningmapa
Lama, Kanjur Rinpoche, and other members of his family to a sort of
"little Shambhala" called, in Tibetan, Pemaköd and located between
Assam and Tibet. In 1911–12, Jedrung Thinlay Chaba Jungney Rin-
poche, Kanjur Rinpoche's teacher, wrote a book called *The Bright Torch
Guide to the Path to the Secret Land of Pemaköd*. The first part of the book,
describing how to go there, is based on revelations by Padmasambhava.
The second part is Jedrung Rinpoche's own description of "the impor-
tant land of Pemaköd and all its wonders."

In this book Jedrung Rinpoche prophesied (some forty years before
the event) that in the Dragon Year (1951) part of Tibet would be
destroyed and its time of intense suffering begin. There would be fam-
ines and wars which would intensify in the Horse Year (1953) and
many would die. The rich would not be able to enjoy their wealth, and
the poor would have no home. Both would think about leaving "tomor-
row," but would be unable to move. Those who did not leave within
five years of the Horse Year (i.e., by 1958) would be "chained by the
lassoes of the devils. Then, even if they wished to escape, there would
be no way to do so, and two years later all exits would be closed."
Jedrung Rinpoche thus urged his followers (and any others who would
listen to him) to "decide in good time to go to Pemaköd and mean it in
the depths of their hearts."

The pilgrim bound for Pemaköd should know that it is no ordinary

Journey to the Land of the Immortals.

land, but one having not only an outer aspect but also inner and secret dimensions. To discover them the aspirant must "move inside progressively." The way is fraught with danger: there are wild animals, poisonous snakes and other terrors. But from such perils the sincere pilgrim is protected. When one reaches "the inner land," everything is transformed.

There are precise instructions for those who decide to go. As a kind of Tibetan *Pilgrim's Progress,* it shows how each stage of the journey has a corresponding spiritual aspect and must be prepared for by appropriate prayers and penances. *conscious suffering.*

In 1954, having decided that the time had come to move to Pemaköd, Kanjur Rinpoche took his family from Tibet to the southeast border area and started looking for the southern entrance to the external Pemaköd. Using Jedrung Rinpoche's account as a guide, they went up a river valley into a gorge that had to be crossed several times on improvised bridges over deep chasms. To make one of these bridges, a certain tree had to be cut down and an axe was found near by, just as the text indicated it would be. Another time they were able to rope their way across the river using an iron ring already fitted into the rock, again as the guide book instructed. Finally, they came to the outer Pemaköd, to the source of the white milk river they had been following, where they found a magnificent waterfall. After a few days of prayer and meditation, the waterfall stopped of its own accord and a deep cave appeared that penetrated into the body of the Vajra Yogini mountain. The way was open.

Once they had all reached the outer Pemaköd, Kanjur Rinpoche left his family behind and, taking only his servant, went into the cave. It turned into a tunnel and three miles later opened on the inner Pemaköd. *moves locate it?* Here they found themselves in an extraordinary landscape completely surrounded by snow peaks. High on the mountain there was every kind of medicinal herb; on the lower slopes, vegetables, grains, cotton, fruits were all growing of their own accord, and they had only to be harvested by those who needed them. Even in the outer Pemaköd, Pema Wangyal remembers finding one large fruit that he had never seen anywhere else and that was sufficient to feed five people. And inside, as his father later related, the atmosphere was extraordinary: the birds sang mantras and

see "the psychic power of animals"

the results of a year's spiritual practice could easily be obtained in a single night. The inner Pemaköd had a magical effect on the old servant. Previously a headstrong, violent man, he returned completely transformed in character. Although they had spent three weeks inside, it had seemed to them only one or two days.

Having completed their pilgrimage to Pemaköd at the time indicated by his teacher, Kanjur Rinpoche and his family then moved south to India and thus escaped the fate of those who were still in Tibet.

My quest has revealed a clear common tradition about Shambhala, emanating from Tibet and Central Asia. It seems that either a real Shambhala exists in those remote fastnesses or that there is (or was) a center from which the Shambhala teaching and myth originated. Undeniably it carries an energy of truth that speaks to the heart.

The more one examines the Shambhala legend the more one is struck by its underlying universality, which can be said to be rooted in the ancient concept of a world or universal center. Thus, in most representations, the mystical city, the center, is depicted as being built on a hill, or "cosmic mountain," that in Tibetan iconography stands for "the center of the world." This notion of a world center was taken for granted in all ancient cultures. Everything important had to be centered and oriented—not only the temple, but the kingdom, the palace, the village, down to the most modest house or tent, and including, of course, the individual self.

Tibetan Buddhist sources show the sky as an eight-spoked wheel and the earth as an eight-petaled lotus. This scheme of the wheel is the mandala of the *Kalachakra Tantra,* one of the most esoteric of Tibetan teachings, which is said to be a revelation given to the King of Shambhala directly by the Buddha. The function of the *Kalachakra Tantra* is to lead us back to the concept of the center: it teaches us symbolically how to use a knowledge of the wheel of time—for *chakra* means "wheel" and *kala* means "time"—to get out of time, and thus escape the decay that is the common lot of all creatures caught in the cycle of mortality. The way out is through the center, through the timeless hub that is still while everything about it is in motion. All beings, teaches the *Kalachakra Tantra,* can be placed somewhere on the wheel of time, and all move more or less rapidly depending on whether they are nearer or farther from the hub. Those rare beings at the hub itself know only stillness and silence—in a state emptied of all but the plentitude of joy.

In the teaching of the *Kalachakra Tantra,* then, Shambhala is the abode of those who have found their way to the center. It is a timeless place in the literal sense, and it has been argued that since space-time is a continuum, it must be a placeless place as well. We are reminded of the parallel Persian legend, in which it is related that the doors of heaven at the top of the cosmic mountain open onto *Nā-Kojā-Abād,* which literally means "nowhere place." From that center, which is timeless and placeless, the 25th Rigden, or King of Shambhala, will ride forth at the end of this cycle of time to restore the authentic teachings of the Buddha to a disoriented world.

Shambhala continues to function today as a crucial energizing myth. As prod and guide, it teaches us that the inner search and the outer search must ultimately and paradoxically be one. We must go out to seek, even if finally what we need to find is at home. The Shambhala legend shows us, in an age addicted to quick solutions, that the road to fulfillment, perfection, heaven is arduous and unending but not an illusory hope. It sets us on a hero's quest which is as universal as here and now, the hub of the great wheel.

It is a tenet of every tradition—whether Chinese or Tibetan, Hebrew or Christian, Hindu or Sufi—that something exists in the innermost recesses of our being that is free from the limitation of time and space; it is the dimension that links us with what is eternal and transcendent. On that central axis turns the temporal world. The Shambhala we are searching for—provided we set out—lies within each of us and at the same time beyond all that is finite and measurable.

As I was finishing this article, a friend in the Iranian Ministry of Foreign Affairs told me a story about the famous Mullah Nasser Eddin that seems curiously apt. Once the Mullah was visiting a village in Anatolia where there lived a rival teacher who wanted to expose the Mullah to ridicule by asking him a question that could not be answered. Accordingly, he approached the Mullah when there were many people standing about, and said: "Tell me, learned Master, where is the center of the world?" The Mullah smiled and pointed to the ground. "The center of the world," he said, "is precisely the spot where I now am standing." When the rival protested that there was no proof of this whatever, the Mullah answered, "If you think you know better, go and measure the world and find the center yourself."

COMMON MIRACLES

Peter Matthiessen

In the farthest part of the Beaverkill Valley, near the end of the dirt road, an old logging trail turns off to the north, climbing two miles or more through hardwood forest to a place where the light changes. Here the trees east of the trail give way to mountain meadow of granite and wild flowers; in deep woodland to the west a brook is running. The brook falls from a stone dam, and beyond the dam lies a black lake that stretches away to a point where mountains meet. This hidden lake, in the heart of a fourteen-hundred-acre tract enclosed almost entirely by state forest, is the highest in the Catskill Mountains. The Lenapi Indians must have had a name for it, or perhaps it had no name at all, but today it is known as Beecher Lake, after James Beecher (the brother of Henry Ward Beecher and Harriet Beecher Stowe), who liked to retreat to this wild place in the late nineteenth century. In 1971, due to a series of remarkable circumstances, the Beecher Lake tract was acquired by the Zen Studies Society, for the site of the International Dai Bosatsu Zendo. That year the wild beaver for which the Beaverkill was named returned to Beecher Lake, only weeks before the ground was broken for the building.

With my wife Deborah, I visited Dai Bosatsu a few weeks after the property had been acquired; we were escorting Soen Roshi, then abbot of Japan's great Ryutaku Monastery, and his disciple, the monk Tai-San (now Eido Roshi). The small miracles that play about Soen Roshi were much in evidence on this visit, and although I had met both these Zen masters in 1968, my formal commitment to Zen practice began with this first visit to Dai Bosatsu three years later.

In January of 1972, Deborah died of cancer; today her ashes lie in the south meadow. In early spring of that same year, I attended the first

25

sesshin at Dai Bosatsu. Before the new building was completed, they had been held in the old Beecher Lake lodge that now serves as a guest house.

These "outdoor notes" derive from the *sesshins* of 1974, which took place mostly in the still-unfurnished monastery.

Formal *sesshin*—a week-long silent retreat—is based upon ten to twelve hours of sitting meditation every day; in warm weather, there are also work *sesshins* in which some of the meditation periods are devoted to work around the monastery. In the brief rest periods, a large bronze Buddha in the shadow of rock and hickory across the lake may be visited by woodland path or by canoe; and all around, the mountains hold what Melville called "that profound silence, the only voice of God."

March Sesshin

Snow flurries come in a white smoke as we draw near the mountains, and in the woods that shut away the outside world, the snow is thick. It falls in darkness as *sesshin* begins, as if to purify the world and shroud the past. The season withdraws from spring into deep winter. But Dai Bosatsu is a home of weather, ever changing, and by morning the white ice of the lake sparkles in the sun.

Deer tracks lead through white woods to the Buddha; an owl hoots at the north end of the pond.

A white limb.
Owl
Shifting thick feathered feet—
    snow falls on snow.

In the evening rest, I go to the south meadow, and stand before the unmarked granite boulder. On the frozen road come footsteps, and in the late winter sun—the days are longer now—I am joined by Soen Roshi, in thin robes and low black shoes that fill with snow. Is this where Deborah is buried? I nod. We chant there, in the silence of the mountain. Then we retrace our footsteps to the road, and standing on the bridge over the dam, chant again into the winter sun, low in the trees. Then the Roshi returns along the road, a small brown figure, the lone monk of ages. Moved, I bow, although he would ignore this: Soen Roshi never says good-bye. By next evening it is snowing once again, and standing on the bridge, breathing with the mountains in the dusk, my thought dissolves, my head becomes transparent, and snow blows through the space where it had been.

In the bright snow outside the kitchen, crisp jays and chickadees share this first day of spring. Two years ago, in winter dusk, as I set out to dig Deborah's grave in the south meadow, a chickadee came from this tree to light on the handle of my pick, and afterward, in stone-filled earth that was locked in snow and ice, the pick sank without hindrance into the one soft place among the stones where her urn would lie.

Across the wind, an early redwing sings, undaunted, though its forage lies beneath yesterday's snow. In the long sittings, I am having pain, and the fragile bird's acceptance of hard going gives me courage.

> Torn redwing,
>> blown to the white birch by the white lake,
>>> sings
> *blackbird!*

Each evening I go to Deborah's grave and listen to the wind in the dark pines; the voices of wild geese pass overhead, from south to north.

Work Sesshin: June

With Soso, whom I knew first at Ryutaku-ji, I work on a forest trail along the shore, exploring ways to span the swamp streams at the beaver pools; he tells me a funny story of *sesshin* at Ryutaku-ji, when he had entered the transparent stillness of *samādhi.* Mysteriously at first, then violently, the world began to tremble, and realizing that he was on the threshold of *kensho*—the "glimpse of enlightenment" that Zen students hope for—he tried desperately to empty his mind, *not to think at all,* for thought is an impediment to seeing. But soon it became impossible to ignore the shouts, the slap of running feet, and he looked up to find himself alone in the great hall; the monks had fled. What was happening was no *kensho* but a real earthquake, and resting a moment by the lake, we laughed; that earthquake might have brought about a *kensho,* too!

Near the place on the lake path, there is now a sign:

Ten years searching in deep forest
At last, great laughter by the lake edge.*

Later, we build bridges, to finish a rough circuit of the lake. Spotted newts are everywhere, orange on land and greenish in the water. A teal like a swift leaf hooks down between the trees into the beaver pools at the north end, and at dusk a wood thrush tries its flute notes in the silence.

In clear still evenings, the trout leap from the black mirror; bats, swallows, fish hunt insects in the air.

A half-day to myself: I climb the west ridge and work my way around the mountains, toward the east. In the cool shadows of high forest stands an elegant woodland grass, just one blade, solitary, still, as if caught listening.

In the meadow, a brown-spotted frog awaits me, transfixed on a warm rock. Shifting flat stones to make a rock path to the grave, I find small snakes—two adult red-bellies, young water snakes, young black-snakes—and make a small snake terrarium for the kitchen. Returning the creatures to the meadow at week's end, I find a beautiful green snake killed on the road.

Work Sesshin: August

The newts are returning to the water, and hang suspended at all depths in the black pond. Each day the deer drift to the lake edge, red does and the shy fawns, and the beaver are active, rebuilding their lodges for the coming winter; at dusk, one leaves a long delicate wake as it swims north. On the first night, I sleep outside, under a sky live with shooting stars and brown bats that flicker from the eaves.

Zenrin Koshu (fifteenth century)

28

Common Miracles

We clear the windfall in the woods, burn brush; at the Gate House, we unload a cargo of beautiful Tasmanian oak that will become the monastery floor. I bake bread, fetch milk from the Barnhart farm, and carve and sand a pair of cedar chopsticks. One evening I walk with Shinsho to the small lake up the logging road, to the west; one night I walk down to the Gate House, surprising a bobcat on the moonlit road.

Goldfinches blowing
In the tall gold black-eyed susans
   —south summer wind!

September Sesshin

The weathers change, clouds blow in mists across the mountain pond. I pick blueberries in the waiting meadow. At twilight, a wild wind spins the lake, and rain and thunder come: *sesshin* begins.

In rest period, each morning, I slip the canoe from the grassy bank and drift along the lake. Red autumn leaves of the swamp maple float on a black mirror. After three days of *sesshin*, everything is extra-ordinary, everything has returned to its true nature—the leaping fish, the stillness of the trees, a dead newt, pale belly up and side by side with a pale dead leaf on the dark bottom. A beaver, like a spirit of the lake, raises its head only yards away, as water pours from the high blunt snout, the coarse-haired head . . . SLAP!—All is still again. Where the creature vanished, there is only a spreading circle in the silence.

Days pass, and the beavers become tame, as if sensing a quiet in my silhouette that was not there before. Yet the ringing and luminosity of the first days of *sesshin* seem to have vanished, as if an intensity had gone. Or is it that I grow accustomed to a fresh way of seeing, and take it now for ordinary perception? As is said in Zen, the mountain is the mountain; then the mountain becomes much more than the mountain; and now the mountain is the mountain once again.

In the night window of the zendo, a full moon appears among the clouds that cross the eastern ridge. The moon comes. The moon goes. A white moth comes out of the night; the white moth goes.

Square

The stars grow colder, and a mist shrouds the lake each morning until the Indian summer sun burns it away. At the north end, a feeding beaver lifts its forepaws from the water, calmly observing, and the trees observe me, too, in red-gold light. I go ashore on the far bank, and removing my robe, swim out into the shining mist.

Early September: a heavy rain at night, clear blue at dawn. *Sesshin* has passed. Open to the world, I wash lettuce by the waterfall. Before leaving, I sit beside the lake with Eido Roshi. "Who is it that is looking at the clouds?" he says. "Do you know who?" Laughing, we lie back in the warm grass and ask this of the clouds in the blue sky.

THE PRISONERS

Edwin Bernbaum

I stood on the ruins of a Nepalese fort, watching the setting sun dissolve into a yellow murk of dust and heat over the plains that I would have to return to the next day. Somewhere far behind me, toward Tibet, were the clean white peaks I had come to see but failed to glimpse for the clouds. Where was that world of clarity and freedom I was looking for high in the Himalayas?

A lone palm, out of place on this ridge high above the jungle of the Terai and Indian plains, rattled desolately in the wind, one of its fronds dangling broken. Around it the walls of the fort, built by Gurkhas a century and a half earlier to repel a British invasion, lay broken and crumbling, moldering under grass and earth. Here and there across fallen stones, half-buried in dirt, cannon barrels pointed blindly at the empty sky. Lost and forgotten, who ever came to walk—

"Namaste."

Two men were walking toward me, picking their way over the walls. One, the shorter, wore Nepali dress—white pants loose around the thighs and tight on the calves, a shirt hanging free from the waist and a black *topi* or cap. He had a curved nose and slender face. The other, tall and strongly built, with curly hair and broad cheeks, had on western slacks and shirt.

I returned their greeting and the shorter man asked in Nepali, "Where are you coming from?"

"From there, near Ramechap," I said, pointing at the next ridge north toward the Himalayas.

"And where are you going?"

"Down to the Terai." I didn't bother to point toward the sickly haze that had now swallowed the sun.

31

"Tell me, please, where is your home?"

"In America. Where is yours?"

"Just below Sindhuli Garhi." Sindhuli Garhi was the village just below the fort.

"And yours?" I asked the taller man.

He crossed his arms and smiled. "Far away from here."

His companion added, "He lives in Sindhuli Garhi now, in the jail."

He must be the jailkeeper, I thought. I looked at the shorter man—he was much younger, about twenty—and asked, "What do you do?"

"I'm a schoolmaster," he answered, straightening his shoulders.

"And you?"

The taller man shrugged. "Nothing."

"Nothing? What do you do in the jail?"

"I am a *kaidi.*"

I pulled my little green Nepali-English dictionary out of my pocket and looked up the word: the entry for *kaidi* read "prisoner." That must be wrong, I thought with a frown, and looked up the word for warden or jailkeeper but couldn't find it. I must have heard it wrong—perhaps the Nepali for prisoner and jailer were very close. I turned back to the taller man. "What did you say you were?"

"A *kaidi.*"

"*Kaidi?*"

"Yes."

"Don't you guard the jail?"

"No." He was smiling at my confusion.

The schoolmaster, who had been peering around my shoulder at the dictionary, said, "He stays in the jail."

"But then, what is he doing out here?"

"Oh, he can go out during the day."

"He's a *kaidi* and he can?"

"Yes, he's the *Mukhya* of the prisoners."

I flipped through the dictionary to *mukhya:* it meant "chief or headman." I looked at the word with disbelief.

The *Mukhya* said, "I have to sleep in jail at night."

"Yes, the warden lets him out during the day but he must come back to be locked up at night—and it's time for him to be back now," the schoolmaster added.

The Prisoners

The sun had set and the sky was gray with twilight. The *Mukhya* glanced at the darkness spreading from the walls and said, "Come with us to the village; we will find you a place to stay tonight."

As we stumbled over stones in the gloom the schoolmaster explained, "You see, the prisoners elect a chief and then the warden is allowed to let him go free during the day."

"And the other prisoners?"

"Oh, they have to stay in jail all the time—they are serving sentences."

"But why don't you . . . uh, leave?" I asked the *Mukhya*.

He shrugged. "I have friends and I like it here. Why should I want to escape?"

It seemed too absurdly reasonable to believe and I remained unsure that I was understanding their Nepali, although they spoke clearly enough.

Sindhuli Garhi was draped across a saddle on the ridge below the fort. Its main street, a path, meandered along the ridge crest between houses roofed with thatch and plastered with red and white dung. Women in *phariyas,* sheet dresses with red sashes wound about the waist, were climbing up from a spring below the village with jugs of water propped on their hips. A few small children wearing only shirts, their rear ends powdery with dust, were playing outside the houses. A couple of water buffalo, looking greasy and reptilian, lolled beside a teashop, where some porters in loincloths were crouched puffing on a water pipe. (*kind of mindi"*)

The *Mukhya* ducked into the teashop and spoke with a man tending the fire. After a few words the man followed him back out and the *Mukhya* said, "Here, this man will take your pack to the policeman's house where you will stay tonight."

Without waiting for thanks he said good-bye and hurried off into the twilight; the schoolmaster pressed his hands into a prayer-like gesture of farewell and followed him. I stood wondering who they really were and how much I had really understood.

The man led me down a stone pathway across a rice terrace and into a house. We climbed a ladder to the second floor and he put my pack on a bed—a table padded with a thin cotton mattress. "They will cook rice for you at the teashop," he said and quickly left.

33

I crossed the room, stepping over cracks between the floorboards, and looked out the window: it faced north toward the Himalayas but gray clouds covered the view. I had hoped to glimpse the snow peaks at nightfall when the sky sometimes clears. But I couldn't even see the next ridge of the foothills. There's nothing, I thought, nothing.

There was nothing in the room either but the bed and darkening gloom. I looked over my pack to make sure everything was there and groped back down the ladder. Outside, men were smoking *bidis* and chatting, while inside their women cooked dinner. A group of boys dashed past, laughing and shouting, and somewhere in the distance a baby began to cry.

Hearing the sound of music coming from a large building I walked toward it. A path led between a fence and a wall to a door with iron bars. It was the prison. I peered in: beyond another door a group of prisoners were singing and dancing in a courtyard. An emaciated man in a *lungi,* a sheet wrapped around his waist and hanging straight to his ankles, was playing a drum slung across his stomach and swaying from step to step. Several other prisoners were following him, singing a gay Nepali song, while the rest, twenty or thirty, clapped in time to the beat. The drummer picked up the tempo and the dancers' feet darted faster, kicking up dust. The singing and clapping whirled up into a frenzy of shouting and smacking that suddenly came to a stop.

The warden, who had been in the courtyard watching the dance, slipped his hand through the bars of the inner door and opened it with a key dangling from his waist. After passing through and locking the door behind him, he saw me and said, "Ah, *namaste,* Sahib. Come watch from here."

I started to tell him I could just as easily watch from outside but he simply opened the door and ushered me in. I hung back in the dark, away from the inner door, not wanting to disturb the dance which had begun again. The warden, however, nudged me closer. He was a plump man with a tiny mustache. The keys to the prison hung on a large ring attached to his belt but he treated them like housekeys, as if nobody would ever think of grabbing them.

The *Mukhya* suddenly appeared out of the crowd and rushed over to the inner door. With a pleased smile, "You have come to visit us,

34

come in!" He glanced at the warden, who added, "Yes, go ahead."

The warden unlocked the door and before I could object I found myself in the courtyard. The lock snapped shut behind me. Was I caught? What if they refused to let me out, who would ever find me here? I looked for the warden but he had gone off to get something. I glanced nervously around the prison and noted with relief that I could easily jump onto the low roof running around the courtyard and scramble over it.

The warden reappeared, unlocked the door and came in to join us with the keys hanging invitingly at his waist. There were no guards; why didn't the prisoners mob him and open the door? In fact why hadn't they already escaped over the roof? I looked around at their faces, messy with stubble, but their eyes showed not the slightest thought of escape—it seemed the farthest thing from their minds. And yet among them there were surely housebreakers, robbers and murderers.

The *Mukhya* took me by the arm and said with a tone of pride, "Let me show you around our prison."

We walked over to a doorway framing a black pit, which he ushered me into. "This is where we sleep." I could dimly make out benches littered with greasy blankets. A stench of sweat and stagnant air overwhelmed me and I mumbled a nicety and hurried back out, breathing deeply to flush the foul air out of my lungs.

The prisoners, some in tatters, some in newer clothes, followed us to the kitchen, the next stop on the tour. The cook, wiping his nose with a grimy hand, was stirring a pot of grayish rice. There was an aroma of rotting garbage. The *Mukhya* greeted him but didn't bother to ask what was for dinner.

Once again we emerged into fresh air—the dirt courtyard looked to me more and more like a garden. What if a man had to stay inside all the time? I shuddered and turned to the *Mukhya*, who pointed to another doorway and said, "Those are the women's quarters. They stay inside."

"Are they prisoners too?"

"Some of them. The rest are prisoners' wives."

The prisoners gathered around and eagerly began to ask the questions usually asked on Nepali trails: "Where are you going? Where are

Arthur Tress

you coming from?" I started to ask the same questions in return but
suddenly realized that these people weren't coming from anywhere nor
going anywhere. I halted in awkward silence.

But they went on. A stout man wearing sandals and a *topi* asked,
"Where is your home?"

"America." I hesitated, eyeing him—he looked like a government
official who had been caught embezzling funds—and asked, "Where is
yours?"

He pointed north toward the Himalayas and said, "The village of
Tose, five days' walk from here."

"Is that in the Himalayas?" I asked with sudden interest.

"They are farther north."

"Do you ever go up there, to Solu Khumbu near Mount Everest?"

He smiled. "No, I have no reason to go."

The other prisoners were watching us, listening intently to our con-
versation. The walls of the prison were tight and gray around them. I
stopped in embarrassment.

The cook began to bang on a pot and I hurriedly asked, "What do
you eat?"

"Rice, bad rice."

"Nothing else, no *dal?"* I was referring to a lentil and pea mush
poured over rice.

He shook his head. "We never have any."

The sky was dark now and I could no longer make out faces in the
dusk. A fire burned in the kitchen, casting a glow into the courtyard and
making me aware of the steamy smell of boiling rice. Glancing at the
bars of the inner door I said to the *Mukhya,* "My food must be ready
at the teashop. I should go."

At an order from the *Mukhya* the prisoners dispersed and he led me
to the door. He pressed my hand and smiled at me. I felt a spasm of guilt
at being free to go, as though I were taking some unfair privilege, and
mumbled good-bye. Then the warden unlocked the doors and I left the
prison, looking back to see the *Mukhya* wave in farewell.

Walking slowly up the path I mused over the friendliness of the
prisoners and their reluctance to escape. Was it more than reluctance?
Were they, like the *Mukhya,* happy there? Didn't they realize that they
were in prison, and could escape whenever they wished? If I were in

their position, I would be long gone. Or would I? Why was I going back down to the plains? Why had they been so friendly to me, treating me like one of them? Was I in some way like them—a prisoner who didn't really want to escape? Somewhere behind me the drumming began again and a prisoner started to sing. I glanced back at the prison and beyond it toward the plains, invisible in the darkness. At that moment I realized the nature of my predicament.

Prescription:

① *To realise that you're = prison.*

② *To know that you can escape (ransom?*

③ *To have the conforintion of escape*

GILGAMESH

The Search for Eternal Life

Introduction

*The climactic portion of the ancient Epic of Gilgamesh may not be unfamil-
iar to the reader: it is something of a school text and has received passing
homage from many of us—often in the first year of college when the full
weight of life was still largely unknown, and the extraordinary precision
of meaning in the epic escaped us. It is in a special class of most ancient
artifacts, with the cave paintings at Lascaux, for example, that bear witness
simply and movingly to the human condition and permit us to study
ourselves through analogies that far surpass our subjective niche in time.*

*The epic as we have it is translated from fragmentary clay tablets
found in the palace library of the Assyrian king Ashurbanipal (Nineveh,
seventh century B.C.) and from fragmentary Babylonian sources dating as
far back as the second millennium B.C.; scholars conjecture that the tale
was compiled from oral sources in the course of the third millennium. The
strands woven into a continuous narrative thus reach beyond the eras we
know, but, strange to say, some of the characters, incidents and locales in
the epic have survived in folktales that we feel to be our own: the garden
of the gods visited by Gilgamesh, with its golden trees and leaves of precious
gems, is not different from the garden crossed by the Twelve Dancing
Princesses. The perennity of so many elements in the epic cannot help but
alert us to the presence of some magic here, of some whole wisdom known
to our forefathers of which we have only fragments.*

see 'Screts of the lost Races".
(eric. Nowberry)

39

The tale is one of search—Gilgamesh's search, after the shock of the death of his closest friend, for the secret of immortality. The cosmos in which Gilgamesh moves is the one that in some form or other all traditional heroes belong to. The search is long, of course, routed past a forbidding gate, through the darkness sealed beneath a mountain, through the garden of the gods where the hero is interviewed by several deities and only reluctantly helped to continue, and thence over the ocean of death in the company of a ferryman who repeatedly urges Gilgamesh to pole the ferry forward. Finally the hero reaches the object of his quest, Utnapishtim, the Babylonian Noah who alone among men knows the secret of immortality. This "Noah" is far from generous, as the reader will discover, and only through the compassionate intervention of Utnapishtim's wife does Gilgamesh leave their hermitage with something other than a remarkable suit of clothes that will, he is told, remain fresh for the entire return journey. The intervention of the woman, like so much else in the tale, may seem specific to this story and perhaps insignificant until it is remembered that "she" often intervenes in the hero's quest and by so doing intimates a law of relationship: in **The Life of Milarepa,** *for example, the twelfth-century* A.D. *Tibetan tale of religious search, it is the guru's wife who encourages the overwhelmed would-be "chela" each time Marpa the Translator refuses to take him as a pupil. The Gilgamesh epic thus relates to the whole literature of search, and can touch us directly, for the demands upon this hero are often enigmatic analogies to the demands still experienced by people today. For example, Gilgamesh is asked to cut 120 poles in the forest, each to be used for one stroke only as he punts over the ocean of death, and dropped as soon as it has served its purpose. Stray interpretative thoughts and objections struggle together in the reader's mind—that this is wasteful of good wood, and at the same time necessary because Gilgamesh was not to permit even a drop of death's water to touch him—until one suddenly realizes the sheer necessity, inherent to any quest, of this kind of challenge. Here it centers on the requirement for complete renewal at every stage of the search, expressed through an image so grandiose that it is nearly absurd. But it was through such paradoxes that ancient man was, perhaps,* *most certain of catching the attention of his audience and passing knowledge onward.*

The concluding portion of the epic has been retold by Paul Jordan-Smith, using transcriptions from the oldest sources available—the Sumerian, Akkadian and Babylonian versions—as well as the scholarship of Samuel Noah Kramer, N. K. Sandars and others.

Gilgamesh fails in the end, returns to his city empty-handed, but the story is telling us that neither success nor failure is of any account: only the search matters. That Gilgamesh has lived so long in the minds of men is evidence of this.

Roger Lipsey

In despair Gilgamesh paced back and forth beside the body of his friend Enkidu. Bitterly he wept, and streaked his face with ashes; he tore off his garments and dressed himself in the pelts of wild beasts. Deep in his heart he cried, "How can I rest, how can I be at peace? Behold Enkidu, my brother and my companion: what he is now, that will I be some day. Because I am afraid of death, I must search for Utnapishtim, whom men call the Faraway, for he has entered the assembly of the gods. Him I will seek, and learn from him the secret of eternal life."

This he said, deep in his heart. Then, crossing the wilderness, traveling over the plains and deserts, Gilgamesh went forth, seeking Utnapishtim, whom the gods saved from the Flood, setting him down in Dilmun, in the garden of the sun. To him they gave eternal life.

Long was the path through the wilderness that Gilgamesh took towards the land of Dilmun. By day he traveled, and by night. When he reached the mountain passes, he made his camp. For a time, he stared into the embers of his fire, remembering his friend Enkidu, and then he slept. But in the night he awoke from a dream and beheld a strange sight: in the moonlight were lions, leaping and playing, glorying in life. Gilgamesh seized his sword and fell upon them, like an arrow from a taut bowstring, and he vanquished them, he destroyed and scattered them.

In the morning, he rose and went his way. Climbing among the foothills toward the mountain passes, he came at length to the great mountain Mashu, which guards the rising and setting of the sun. At its gate stand the Scorpion-People, the dragons who guard the passes, and whose glance is death. To them came Gilgamesh, King of Uruk. For a moment only did he shield his eyes; then he collected his thoughts and went forward.

When they saw him coming toward them undaunted, the Man-Scorpion said to his mate, "This one who comes toward us is flesh of the gods." His mate replied, "Two-thirds of him is god, but one-third is man." Then the Man-Scorpion called to Gilgamesh, child of the gods, "Who is this who comes to us, weary and worn out with traveling? I see a man whose body is covered with the pelts of wild beasts, whose face is streaked with ashes. The flesh of the gods is in his body, but despair is in his heart. You have come a long way: why are you here? What do you seek that you will risk death in the mountain passes?"

"It is I, Gilgamesh, King of Uruk, who have come here," said Gilgamesh to the Man-Scorpion. "Why should I not be weary and worn out with traveling? Why should not my cheeks be drawn and my face be downcast? Why should not my heart be full of despair and my face full of anguish? There is woe in my heart, for Enkidu, my brother and companion, is dead. He was the axe at my side, my shield's strength: together we slew the monster Humbaba, together we slew the Bull of Heaven. Enkidu is dead: the hands of the gods struck him down, and the judges of the underworld, the Annunaki, took him below. By his side I sat and watched death creep through his limbs, and I became afraid for myself: I, Gilgamesh, King of Uruk, who slew Humbaba and the Bull of Heaven, fear death.

"Now I seek Utnapishtim, the Faraway, whom the gods saved from the Flood, whom the gods set down in Dilmun to live forever: surely he knows the secret of eternal life, surely he can answer the questions that torment me, surely he will tell me what I must do so that the fate of my friend will not be my own. That is why mine is the face of one who has made a long journey, that is why my face is burned with the heat and the cold."

"No one has made the passage through Mount Mashu," replied the Man-Scorpion. "Twelve leagues the way lies in darkness, beneath the mountain. Would you go that way? There is no other. No man has made the journey. There is no light there, the presence of Shamash does not find a way in."

Gilgamesh answered, "Though it be in darkness and cold, though it be in sorrow and pain, in sighing and weeping, I will go: open the gate of the mountain."

Then the Man-Scorpion said to the King of Uruk, "Gilgamesh, I see that in your heart you are determined to go, whatever the risk. Therefore, King of Uruk, I will open the mountain passes, I will open the gate to Mount Mashu. May your aim light your way in the dark passages, may you find what you seek, may your feet carry you safely back. Go forward! The gate of Mashu is open."

When Gilgamesh heard this, he followed the path into the mountain. As he entered the pass, the darkness closed around him. One league he travels; dense is the darkness, there is no light: he can see nothing ahead and nothing behind him. Two leagues he travels; dense is the darkness, there is no light: he can see nothing ahead and nothing behind him. Three leagues he travels; dense is the darkness, there is no light: he can see nothing ahead and nothing behind him. Four leagues, five leagues, six leagues he travels; dense is the darkness, there is no light: he can see nothing ahead and nothing behind him. After he has traveled seven leagues, dense is the darkness and there is no light: he can see nothing ahead and nothing behind him. Eight leagues he travels, and gives a great cry: for dense is the darkness, there is no light: he can see nothing ahead and nothing behind him. Nine leagues he travels, and now he feels the north wind upon his face; but dense is the darkness, there is no light: he can see nothing ahead and nothing behind him. After he has traveled ten leagues, the end is near. After he has traveled eleven leagues, the gleam of sunrise shines upon him. After he has traveled twelve leagues, he bursts forth from the mountain, and the light of Shamash streams down upon him.

In this way Gilgamesh found his way to the garden of the gods, where the trees are of gold, their branches of silver and their fruit of precious gems. The leaves are lapis lazuli, and grapes of carnelian hang upon the vines. Weary and worn out with traveling, Gilgamesh sat upon the shore, his head bowed down upon his arms. Shamash saw him, saw the King of Uruk, saw the labors and the weariness of the man dressed in the pelts of wild beasts. And Shamash felt pity for the man. He stood before Gilgamesh and said, "Gilgamesh, whither runnest thou? The life which thou seekest thou wilt not find."

Then Gilgamesh raised his head. He looked at the god and said, "Long have I journeyed in darkness, through the wilderness and over the mountain passes. In darkness I have labored seeking Utnapishtim, the Faraway. Am I to cover my head with earth and sleep the rest of my years? Though I may be no better than a dead man, let me at least look upon the light of the sun."

With her golden bowl she sits in the garden by the edge of the sea: Siduri, the alewife, maker of wine. To her gate came Gilgamesh: from afar she watched him coming. She thought, "Who is this who comes dressed in the pelts of wild beasts? A thief, surely, is this, some brigand who has made his way here," and she rose up to bar the gate. Yet even as the bolt shot home, Gilgamesh lodged his foot in the gate and cried out, "Woman, alewife, maker of wine, why do you bar the gate to me? I will smash your gate, tear down your door, for I am Gilgamesh, King of Uruk. Twelve leagues in darkness have I traveled to come here. You cannot bar the way to me!" Then, pushing aside the gate, he entered the courtyard. Siduri said to him, "Why have you come this way? Are you looking for the wind? Your face is streaked with ashes, and despair is in your heart."

Gilgamesh replied, "Why should I not be weary and worn out with traveling? Why should not my cheeks be drawn and my face be downcast? Why should not my heart be full of despair and my face full of anguish? There is woe in my heart, for Enkidu, my brother and companion, is dead: the hands of the gods struck him down, and the judges of the underworld, the Annunaki, took him below. By his side I sat and watched death creep through his limbs, and I became afraid for myself.

"Now I seek Utnapishtim, the Faraway, whom the gods saved from the Flood, whom the gods set down in Dilmun to live forever: surely he knows the secret of eternal life, surely he can answer the questions

Dino Cavallari

The dark way through Mount Mashu.

that torment me, surely he will tell me what I must do so that the fate of my friend will not be my own. That is why mine is the face of one who has made a long journey, that is why my face is burned with the heat and the cold."

Siduri said to him, "Gilgamesh, whither runnest thou? The life which thou seekest thou wilt not find. When the gods created man, they allotted to him death: life they retained for themselves. As for you, Gilgamesh, fill your belly with food and wine, day and night be merry and dance, feast and rejoice. Put on fresh clothes, bathe in fresh water, cherish the child that holds your hand, and make your wife happy in your embrace: this is the lot of man." *Who men...*

A long time Gilgamesh sat in silence before he spoke. "Woman, how can I rejoice in life when Enkidu, my brother and companion, is dead? What he is now, that will I be some day. Am I to forget my fate? Young woman, you sit by the sea and have looked into the heart of it: tell me now the way to Dilmun, the way to Utnapishtim, the Faraway, that I may ask of him the secret of eternal life. Give me, oh give me directions for the passage over the ocean, or I must wander still further in the wilderness."

Then said Siduri, "Gilgamesh, Gilgamesh: there is no crossing of the Ocean of Death. Whoever has come, since ancient times, has not crossed that sea. The Sun in glory crosses the Ocean, but who besides Shamash can make the passage? Deep are the waters of death, and what will you do when you come to them? But I see that in your heart you are determined to go, whatever the risk. Therefore, I will help you.

"Go down to the woods by the side of the sea. There you will find Urshanabi, the ferryman of Utnapishtim. With him are the holy things, the Ones of Stone. Find Urshanabi, where he sits carving the serpent prow of his boat, and look at him well, and let him see you. Perhaps he will help you cross the waters. If he will not, you must go back. Without his help, there is no way to the land of Dilmun."

When Gilgamesh heard this, he leapt up and ran down to the woods by the side of the sea, his sword in one hand, his axe in the other. He smashed the Ones of Stone that stood in his way. He found Urshanabi, deep in the woods, where he sat carving the serpent prow of his boat, and Gilgamesh said to the ferryman, "Show me the way to Utnapishtim, who lives forever in the land of Dilmun. If the way is possible, even over

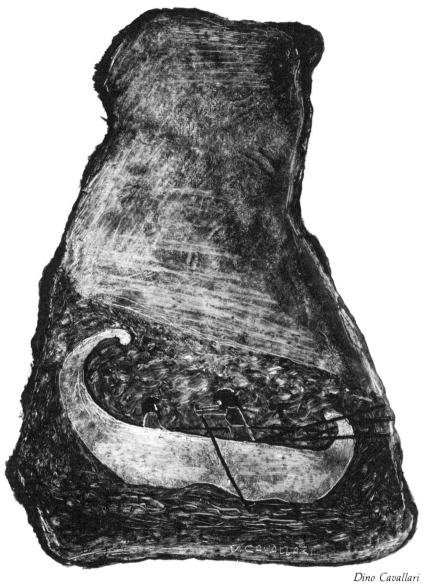

Dino Cavallari

Crossing the Waters of Death.

the waters of death, I will go there, or wander still further in the wilderness."

Urshanabi looked up at him, looked long into the heart of the King of Uruk. He said, "Gilgamesh, your own hands hindered your journey, when you destroyed the Ones of Stone, who protected this boat in its passage. Hard was the way before: now it is almost impossible. The Ones of Stone protected me from the waters of death, they kept the waters from touching me. Now, where is my protection? You must provide it. Else there is no crossing the ocean.

"Go into the woods. With your axe, cut punting poles. Cut one hundred and twenty poles, Gilgamesh, each sixty cubits long. Then paint them with bitumen, cap their ends with ferrules, and when all are ready, bring them here."

When Gilgamesh heard this, he went straightaway into the forest to cut punting poles: one hundred and twenty poles he cut, each sixty cubits in length; he painted them with bitumen and capped them with ferrules, and brought them to Urshanabi. Then, together, they launched the boat.

Swift over the sea ran the ferryman's boat: in three days they covered the distance of a month and a half, and they reached the waters of death that bar the way to Dilmun. Then said Urshanabi to Gilgamesh, "Press on, Gilgamesh: take a pole and thrust it into the sea, but do not let your hands touch the water. Gilgamesh, take a second pole, and a third and a fourth. Gilgamesh, take a fifth pole, and a sixth and a seventh. Now Gilgamesh, take an eighth pole, and a ninth and a tenth. Gilgamesh, take an eleventh pole, and a twelfth." Thus, slowly over the waters of death they punted the boat, and when Gilgamesh had used the one hundred and twentieth pole, there were no poles left. The King of Uruk stripped himself then, and held up his arms like a mast, with his pelts aloft for sails. The wind puffed out his garments and slowly they crossed the waters of death: so did Urshanabi bring Gilgamesh to Dilmun, to the shore where lived Utnapishtim, whom men call the Faraway.

On the far shore of that sea sat Utnapishtim, taking his ease. He raised his eyes to the horizon, and beheld a strange sight: there was the boat of the ferryman, and standing in the prow of the boat a strong man, almost a god, his arms raised for a mast, his raiment flapping in the wind. "Who is this who comes?" Utnapishtim said to himself. "He is no servant of mine. The flesh of the gods is in his body, but despair is in his heart." Then, as the boat came to the shore, he called out, "What is your name, you who come here wearing the pelts of wild beasts, with your face streaked with ashes and despair in your heart? Why have you made the difficult passage with your arms raised like a mast? It is not fatigue that has brought weariness to your bones: tell me the reason for your coming."

As he stepped ashore, Gilgamesh spoke. "I am Gilgamesh, from the House of Anu, King of Uruk. I have made a long journey: why should I not be weary and worn out with traveling? Why should my cheeks not be drawn and my face not be downcast? Why should not my heart be full of despair and my face full of anguish? Enkidu, my brother and companion, is dead. He was the axe at my side, my shield's strength: together we slew the monster Humbaba, together we slew the Bull of Heaven. But the hands of the gods struck him down, and the judges of the underworld, the Annunaki, took him below. By his side I sat and watched death creep through his limbs, and I became afraid for myself. I, Gilgamesh, King of Uruk, who slew Humbaba and the Bull of Heaven, fear death.

"I have come seeking Utnapishtim, the Faraway, whom the gods saved from the Flood, whom the gods set down in Dilmun to live forever: surely he knows the secret of eternal life, surely he can answer the questions that torment me, surely he will tell me what I must do so that the fate of my friend will not be my own."

Utnapishtim said to him, "What lasts forever? Does a man build a house to stand forever? Are contracts sealed for all time? Do brothers divide their inheritance to keep forever? Does hatred persist forever in the land?

"What endures forever? Does the flood-time of the river endure forever? Does the face of the dragon-fly see the face of the sun forever? From the days of old, there is no permanence. The sleeping and the dead, how alike they are! It is as if death were a painting of sleep, and sleep a painting of death. The Annunaki gather together and with Mammetum, the goddess of destiny, they decree the life and death of all creatures. The life of a man unfolds as he lives it; the day of his death is not revealed."

Buddhist Concept.

49

In anger Gilgamesh replied, "A long way have I come, and for what? I thought to find a man prepared for battle, a warrior. Instead, I find a tired old man, taking his ease in the sun. And yet, you are here. Tell me then, how it was that you came to enter the company of the gods, and to possess eternal life?"

Utnapishtim said, "I will reveal to you a mystery, I will tell you a secret of the gods.

> I will tell thee, Gilgamesh,
> Of a mournful mystery of the gods:
> How once, having met together,
> They resolved to flood the land of Shuruppak.
> Clear-eyed Ea, saying nothing to his father, Anu,
> Nor to the Lord, the great Enlil,
> Nor to the spreader of happiness, Nemuru,
> Nor even to the underworld Prince, Enua,
> Called to him the son of Ubara-Tutu;
> Said to him: "Build thyself a ship."

Then did Utnapishtim tell Gilgamesh how he came to survive the "Flood before the Flood," how for six days and nights the ship floated on the sea, and came to rest at last atop a mountain, how the gods relented and took him up with his wife and set him down faraway in the land of Dilmun.

"As for you, Gilgamesh," Utnapishtim concluded, "who will call the gods to assemble for your sake? Who will plead your case that you may find the life for which you seek? But come, let us put it to the test. Only prevail against sleep for six days and seven nights. . . ."

But even as Utnapishtim spoke, sleep like a fog blew upon him, and Gilgamesh closed his eyes. Then Utnapishtim the Faraway said to his wife: "Look at him now, the great hero! This is the man who wishes eternal life! Sleep like a fog blows upon him." Utnapishtim's wife said to him, "Touch and wake him, so that he may return to his own land in peace, so that he may return by the gate through which he came." "All men are deceivers," said Utnapishtim. "Even you he will try to deceive. Therefore, bake bread each day that he sleeps, one loaf each day, and put it beside his head, and mark on the wall the number of days that he sleeps."

So Utnapishtim's wife baked bread that day, and each day thereafter while Gilgamesh slept, and when seven days had passed, Utnapishtim touched the man, and he awoke. "I had hardly slept when you touched and roused me," said Gilgamesh, but Utnapishtim pointed to the loaves of bread and to the marks on the wall.

"Count the loaves, Gilgamesh," Utnapishtim said to him. "Learn how many days you have slept. See, the first loaf is hard, and the second is like leather; the third loaf is soggy, the crust of the fourth has mold; the fifth loaf is mildewed, and the sixth is fresh; and the seventh loaf is still warm from the oven."

"What shall I do?" said Gilgamesh. "Where shall I go? The thief in the night has already laid hold of my limbs, death crouches in the corner. Wherever I set my foot, there I find death."

Utnapishtim spoke then to Urshanabi, the ferryman. "Woe to you from this day forth, Urshanabi, for no longer will your boat find harbor on these shores. This man whom you have led here—take him to the washing-place, so that he may freshen his limbs, give him such clothes as will cover his nakedness, and serve him well on his journey home." So Urshanabi took Gilgamesh to the washing-place, and the King of Uruk refreshed his limbs. Then, while he was washing, Utnapishtim's wife said to her husband, "Weary and worn out with traveling came Gilgamesh to these shores. To see you, he has exerted himself to his utmost. Shall he go away empty-handed? Give him something, a small boon to carry back to his own country, that his long search may not be utterly in vain."

Utnapishtim went down to the washing-place, and called to Gilgamesh: "Gilgamesh, King of Uruk, you came to the shores of Dilmun weary and worn out with traveling. You exerted yourself to the utmost to see me. What will you take back with you, that your search will not have been in vain? Gilgamesh, I will reveal to you a secret thing, a mystery of the gods will I tell you. There is a plant, with thorns like a rose, which grows under the water. Its thorns will wound your hands and tear your flesh, but if you succeed in taking it, your hands will hold that which will give you new life." *Punic Rose*

Then Gilgamesh swam to the shore, and tied stones to his feet. He opened the sluice-gates and let the sweet-water current carry him out to the deepest channel. When the stones carried him down to the very bottom, Gilgamesh saw the plant growing, one with thorns like a rose. He seized the plant, and its thorns tore his flesh, but with both hands he took it and, cutting the stones from his feet, he rose to the surface.

Gilgamesh said to Urshanabi, the ferryman, when he climbed into the boat, "Look, my friend! Come and see this marvelous plant. With this may a man win back his lost youth, by its virtue will he regain his strength! This will I take with me to Uruk, and give it to the old men to eat. I will call it, 'Old Men Are Made Young Again,' and when I too at last have eaten it, I will have back all my youth." By the gate through which he had come did Gilgamesh travel to strong-walled Uruk, and Urshanabi went with him. After thirty leagues, they made their camp by a well of cool water.

Gilgamesh wished to wash the dust from his body, and he went down into the well to bathe, leaving the plant by the side of the pool. Deep in the pool there was lying a serpent, and the serpent smelled the sweetness of the flower, and rose out of the water. Quietly it slipped forward toward the plant, and snatched it away. Immediately, the old skin of the serpent fell away and it returned to the well. When Gilgamesh came out of the water, he saw what had happened, and he wept:

> For whose sake have I worn out my limbs, Urshanabi?
> For whose sake has my heart's blood been spent?
> No blessing did I bring to myself or others—
> Only to the serpent underground have I brought good service!

This is the story of Gilgamesh, of the House of Anu, King of Uruk of the strong walls. This was the man who knew all the countries of the world, who saw everything, who knew mysteries and secret things. He went on a long journey, he exerted himself to his utmost, he was weary and worn out with traveling. He brought us a tale of the days before the flood, and he engraved on a stone the whole story.

Gilgamesh

The moon waxes and wanes,
The fish swims to the hook,
The deer discovers the noose:
At the bend, the chariot
Turns and disappears:
One day, the shepherd
Goes into the mountain,
One day the king
Takes to his bed.
Empty sandals
Attest his feet.

retold by Paul Jordan-Smith

A question have I become for myself.

Saint Augustine

If you wish to know the road up the mountain, you must ask the man who goes back and forth on it.

Buddhist text

"This is the way all right," said Monkey. "Look! Just over there is a bridge. That's the right way to Salvation."

Presently Tripitaka came to a notice-board on which was written Cloud Reach Bridge. But it proved, when they came up to it, that the bridge consisted simply of slim tree trunks laid end on end, and was hardly wider than the palm of a man's hand.

"Monkey," protested Tripitaka in great alarm, "it's not humanly possible to balance on such a bridge as that. We must find some other way to get across."

"This is the right way," said Monkey, grinning.

"It may be the right way," said Pigsy, "but it's so narrow and slippery that no one would ever dare set foot on it. And think how far there is to go, and what it's like underneath."

"All wait where you are, and watch while I show you how," cried Monkey. Dear Monkey! He strode up to the bridge, leapt lightly on to it, and had soon slipped across. "I'm over!" he shouted, waving from the other side. Tripitaka showed no sign of following him, and Pigsy and Sandy bit their fingers murmuring, "Can't be done! Can't be done!" Monkey sprang back again and pulled at Pigsy, saying, "Fool, follow me across."

But Pigsy lay on the ground and would not budge. "It's much too slippery," he said. "Let me off. Why can't I have a wind to carry me?"

"What would be the good of that?" said Monkey. "Unless you go by the bridge you won't turn into a Buddha."

Wu Ch'êng-ên, Monkey

THE SEARCH
FOR TRANSFORMATION

D. M. Dooling

What does it mean to search, to be a seeker? It is too big a word to be used lightly, for it has to do with seeing; not that kind of physical seeing which we share with the animals, but an inner perception which is peculiar to the human being and is his highest attribute. Or perhaps I should say his highest *possible* attribute, for not everyone can "see" in this fashion, and certainly not everyone can call himself a seeker. The seeker is humanity's chance to grow, for he is not satisfied, he is not sure of his answers, he has not "come to a conclusion." He looks for more; he is a person with an active question, with a *quest;* in other words, he is a hero.

Perhaps we can only aspire to be seekers; go into training, as it were, in order to become worthy of the title. And to do this seriously, we have to find a question and begin to look, for it is by making a start that one begins to discover what the role of seeker really is and to become what it represents.

With what question shall we begin, then? What do we want to find out, or to find? If we listen only a little, we are aware of some dissatisfaction; something is certainly lacking, something needs to be found—and it doesn't seem to be anything completely new or unknown, but something we have lost, something that belonged to us but that disappeared so long ago we have forgotten it was ever ours. It is a kind of "lost chord" that still resounds in us at moments, and at such moments affirms the wholeness of our own identity.

At the heart of all the traditions there is the recognition of this loss and its possible restoration, a recognition of the return to unity as the destiny of man. The Fall and the exile from Eden speak of it, and the homeward journey of the prodigal son; the marvelous circling dance of the Mevlevi dervishes; the words of the Upanishad: "When I go hence, I shall obtain him." To *return* is the basic human longing. Paradise is man's lost home, so far away in time and space, so diametrically opposite to his daily realities, that he may hope to go back to it only in another life, in another world.

On the one-level plane of existence where most of us live most of our lives, the vision of a transforming destiny, a reunion of myself with myself, has either to be abandoned or reduced to an infantile dream of some purified and ideal existence on the other shore of death. Any connection with an idea of another level must become imaginary, if it starts from a plane of thought dominated by the scientistic dictum that everything must be measured by physical means, in terms of our most primitive functions. By this downward-heading trend of reasoning, the higher must come to the lower, the greater to the less. It is this kind of thinking that takes the symbolism of the religious traditions and of sacred art to be merely an illustration of our bodily experience, instead of what it is: a living representation of truth which our experience only partially reflects. We need to be careful not to confuse the reflection with the fact, like the dwellers in Plato's cave who take for granted that their limited view constitutes the whole possibility of human life and being. If we suspect that there is more, and wish for it, we must find a way of access.

Creation myths from everywhere show how man was produced from the wholeness of God in an incomplete form: "Male and female created He them," and in the Mayan myth, the gods, seeing the original man too nearly perfect, blow mist into his eyes to cloud and limit his vision. Christians call this human incompleteness "sin," a word that comes from the same root as the word *to be* (Indo-European *es,* participial *sont*); but the wisest among them, with St. Augustine, also call it "blessed," for the incompleteness of man's being is his possibility of becoming. This incompleteness, or "imperfection," is what makes him "a little lower than the angels," and yet gives him a higher potential; he is capable of becoming God's son as well as his servant.*

---

*The definition of sin implied by its etymology is borne out by the fact that "imperfect" literally means "unfinished" or "incomplete." Taking the original meaning of "sin" in this sense gives quite a different—and more comprehensible—reading of Paul, I Corinthians 15, 56: "The sting of death is sin; and the strength of sin is the law."

But how is the human potential to be achieved? What we are *in fact* is incompletion, a fraction divided between self-admiration and self-pity. Sometimes this random collection is satisfied with itself as it is, deluded by its apparent accomplishments and confident of its future successes; then dashed by its equally accidental failures, blaming itself and others in an agony of pessimism; always either before or after its own events. Or perhaps at moments these fragments come closer to each other and to the present instant and there is a momentary view of undeveloped capacities, unexplored territory, vistas that are unknown yet reminiscent of something forgotten—and the nostalgia for Paradise arises anew. The chasm is there and the need to bridge it; one is caught between the Clashing Rocks of one's own contradictions—one's own personal Symplegades. This is the human experience, and everywhere we find the symbols of our predicament in all its terror and all its hope. Then, if our desire for wholeness is the beginning of a real search and not simply another song of self-pity, we will look at the images of myth and symbol not as poetic descriptions but as coded messages that could help us to face our danger and perhaps, like the mythic heroes, over-come it.

These "forms of revelation that God in His mercy created," as sym-bols were described by a seventeenth-century artist, are various in appearance, but inevitably interconnected by their original dwelling together in the mind of God. The process of transformation of the fragment that man is into the whole of his origin, his possible return to the home of his father, is a dangerous passage: between "the rocks that clap together" (or the icebergs, or the falling portcullis, or the Cutting Reeds or whatever it may be, depending on the moment and the place where it was rephrased); up through the branches of the Sacred Tree, or on the rungs of the Ladder that reaches to Heaven; through the maze of Minos, or across the rainbow bridge of the Navaho or the Scandina-vian legends. It is a constant retelling of the myth of man's becoming, a becoming that does not happen but must be attained. It is Everyman's quest, but possible only for one who is a seeker and a hero.

The mythic bridge and the perils of its crossing reappear again and again. The rainbow bridge Bifrost of *The Prose Edda* was "of three colors and great strength, made with more cunning and art of magic than any other work of craftsmanship; yet it must be broken, when the sons of

Passing through the Gorge.

Lancelot crossing the Sword Bridge.

Muspell shall go forth harrying and ride it." The rainbow traversed by the Navaho brothers, the Slayers of the Enemy Gods, on the contrary was so fragile that the gods had to harden it with their breath lest the heroes slip through. Lancelot walked on the edge of a sword-blade to reach the country where his lady was held captive; Bodhidharma crossed the ocean of transmigration on a reed. Endless examples could be cited, but what are we really being told? More interesting than the varying forms of the bridge itself is the *how* of its crossing.

The Chinvat Bridge in the Mazdaean tradition was said to be projected from a mountain peak, the peak of judgment, at the center of the world, and on this bridge the soul's final destiny was decided, for it could be reached only after death. At its entrance the righteous soul meets the angel who is his true, fulfilled identity; but the unrighteous soul encounters a hideous creature and is possessed by it. Here some very interesting questions arise. What kind of "death" is really being spoken of? For it hardly seems that the bridge could be reached in any automatic or accidental way. It is "at the center" and "on a mountain peak," the mythic description of the goal of the hero's quest; and the hero, surely, is victorious and alive. So what meaning has *death* here?

Luisa Coomaraswamy, speaking of similar Hindu myths in her definitive essay on the Perilous Bridge, says: "It is not only in a future life that the end of the road can be reached; the shores are but an arrow-shot apart, if one knows what is the 'arrow' and how it must be 'released.' "* She also refers to a West African story in which a man creates a magic bridge with a chain of arrows which he shoots alternately into the near and the far shores; and to the correspondence of this story with American Indian legends of similarly created ladders to heaven. What indeed is the nature of such an arrow? Is it like that of the Japanese master of archery who bade his greatest pupil shoot down a star, and then surpassed the feat by doing the same thing without using either arrow or bow? These "arrows" hint at another kind of speed, directness and power, a "magical" activity that could not be the property of ordinary functioning, but of that which can appear only when ordinary functioning and its governor, the human ego, are no longer in control. Then do

---

*"The Perilous Bridge of Welfare," by Luisa Coomaraswamy, *Harvard Journal of Asiatic Studies*, 8:2 (August 1944): 196–213.

these stories perhaps reveal, by implication, another kind of death—not that of the body, which comes to everyone, but that of the ego, which is earned by few?

But here we must be very careful, for what does it mean that the ego should die? Surely it is a misunderstanding and a diminishing of the symbol to think of the "crossing over" as the leaving behind of one kind of being in order to pass into a "better" one. What can be abandoned if what we are seeking is our own wholeness? I do not think that we can attain a transformed being by simply adding to our virtues and abolishing our vices; and if by "ego" we mean to characterize our selfish human nature, we can never (fortunately) be rid of it. Only what has a merely illusory existence can be discarded without loss to the whole. But if we take "ego" to mean the imaginary importance which my person gives itself, the lie it tells by calling itself "I," this indeed is an image whose "death" is necessary in order that I may become truly and wholly what I am. This *fantasy* must disappear. The selfish human nature, however, must not be "killed" but must remain to be taken into that other nature which has hitherto been overpowered by sleep; it must be transmuted into the strength and substance necessary to establish that Other's rightful supremacy. Indeed, the ego in a certain sense is even the savior of this Other, who needs not only the ego's strength and substance but his very difficulties, errors and inadequacies in order to awaken and respond.

A version of the Chinvat Bridge passed from the Zoroastrian teaching into Islamic folklore as the steep and narrow bridge over Hell called Sirāt, on which the wicked could not keep their footing and plunged into the abyss; but a description quoted by Mrs. Coomaraswamy says that "if the deceased can make the right answers to the questions put to him in the grave, a gate of Paradise is opened for him and he is led onto the bridge and brought over it by an angel, and it will seem to him as soft and level as the palm of the hand." I would compare this to a much more recent work that is yet totally true to the myth, Howard Pyle's *The Garden Behind the Moon*. The boy David, the hero of the story, makes the journey from his home village, where he is neglected and derided as simpleminded, to the Otherworld of the moon and its delightful garden, and finally to another and even more terrible passage into manhood and a hero's adventures. His bridge over the sea to the

63

Weighing the Souls on the Chinvat Bridge.

moon, at the start of his journey, is the path of light that the newly risen moon at its full casts on the waves; at that exact moment he must step out on the wriggling bar of moonlight on the top of one wave and jump to the next, without yielding to fear. His first attempt does not succeed and he is nearly drowned; but on his second try, he manages to jump from wave to wave until he finds himself on a broad path like silver gravel on which he can run easily.

Both these stories seem to indicate something of how the bridge is to be crossed; a note here rings in harmony with our own experience. There is a choice to be made, and we seem to know the taste of that choice—a "right answer," a refusal of weakness that brings a moment of certain knowing, and the road becomes "level" and easy to travel. But one knows well that this must be paid for; we also, like David, have choked on salt water. Access to the bridge can never be easy. In the Zoroastrian myth, one must climb the mountain at the center of the world, and pass through death before, at the entrance of the Chinvat Bridge, the perfected soul can be joined with what Henry Corbin calls its "heavenly I." All the teachings of the bridge speak of difficulty and suffering, for the bridge, of course, is within; it is, in fact, myself, if I can make myself conform to the process and take the risk of situating myself "in between." "Who would be Chief, let him be the bridge," says the *Mabinogion;* and to be Chief, one needs no more followers than one's own unruly selves. It is only within that the battle can take place, the choice be made, the false images vanquished and the seeker incarnated; and until the seeker comes, the angel waits in vain upon the bridge. It is only when seeker and angel clasp hands that the crossing can take place.

Once crossed, we are told, the bridge must disappear for him who crosses it, as the Buddha bade the traveler forget his raft when the other shore was gained. That we need such a warning is evidence of how easily we confuse the inner and the outer. The crossing is within, it is in movement, and it is instantaneous, like the flight of the arrow, like David's leap from wave to wave at the instant of the moon's rising. It exists only in that moment out of time which is *now*, between *was* and *will be;* it is itself the bridge of a different, truer reality between our ordinary view of time past and time to come—the time-sense of our everyday life in which even today is nothing but partly past and partly future. The present is a moment, a flash that always escapes our slow-footed ego-awareness, that exists only for the arrow-swift intuition that belongs to the seeker himself. So of course the bridge must disappear when the crossing is made; it is no longer needed, for both shores are joined, and the separation also has disappeared. The hero has become whole. He has not left one world for another, but found how one is part of the other, and in that liberating relationship has freed himself from all limits and all divisions.

A DIALOGUE BETWEEN ONE AND ZERO

Sōhaku Kobori

Introduction

Sōhaku Kobori exasperates the Western reader. This kind, ever-so-polite Zen Roshi puts the so-called search in question without so much as by-your-leave, without an inch of compromise.

How hard it is to relinquish the cozy belief that one can come other than empty-handed to one's reality. But Kobori, Abbot of Ryōkōin Monastery in Kyoto, makes no bones about the futility of searching with what he calls the "differentiating" intellect.

Bang!—he tells us—you can search all your lifetime through with the ego-centered self, oh you blockhead! But, enter the chaos of the "undifferentiated" and you may get it, you may get it. You may enter the real world, this plain, ordinary, extraordinary world of here and now, which cannot be obtained by discipline alone or expressed through logical exposition.

Like all masters, Kobori clings to the unspoken assumption that deeply embedded in humanity is the awareness of different dimensional possibilities for existence. He attempts through symbols to indicate the experience which cannot be logically contained or expressed through words or formulas. In a sense he is saying that we ourselves are what we are looking for and the only time for the search is now.

He puzzles me. But sometimes, when we meet, we have a good laugh together.

William Segal

Triangle

One: A few weeks ago I chanced to visit an exhibition of Oriental art in the K. Museum. Among the paintings, I noticed one which seemed to me quite simple and fresh—a few persimmons drawn in black ink. Though the arrangement of the fruit was monotonous, the whole produced a somewhat mystical effect and seemed to lead me into an unknown realm. Unfortunately, however, I could not understand the painter's intention. Therefore, the next day I dropped into the home of a Japanese friend to whom, since I have come to know him, I have been attracted by his rare personality and profound thought.

"Do you know the painting exhibit now being held at the K. Museum?" I asked him.

"Yes," he replied.

"Among the paintings on exhibition there I noticed a black and white drawing, of persimmons, I think. Though it was quite simple, the painting attracted me, but its meaning was beyond my understanding. Since seeing it I have been wondering what it means, what its value is. And I am also eager to know something about the Oriental spirit which could produce an art so alien to our styles and traditions. Won't you tell me something about this?"

"Don't wonder about the painting," my friend replied. "It is useless for you to try to discover the meaning of the persimmons through intellectual understanding. If you attempt to do so, you may be led up a blind alley. You had better cease seeking outside for the meaning. You must first of all touch that which you yourself really are. You must begin with the reality within yourself."

At that time I could not quite grasp his meaning. I have been

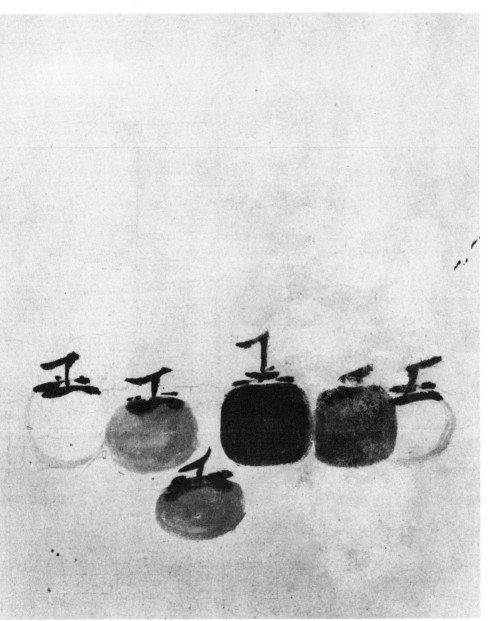

Mokkei

The Six Persimmons.

thinking about what he said to me and, in confusion, have come to you.

Zero: Now I understand the reason for your visit this afternoon. Tell me what is in your mind.

One: I want to know what the persimmons painting means.

Zero: It is just a simple expression of the painter's inner life. The painter is Mokkei, as I remember, a Zen monk who lived during the early part of the Southern Sung dynasty, and who was also a famous painter.

One: Oh, does the painting represent the simplicity of his monkish life, his wearing of black and white clothing? Or do the persimmons, arranged so monotonously, symbolize Zen monks sitting in meditation?

Zero: Absolutely not! You are quite an outsider. The door of the inner life is shut to you, for you are always unconscious of the true fact of life.

One: We generally consider that our daily life consists of material and spiritual elements. Does this differ from what you call the "inner life"?

Zero: You cling to words. When you hear the term "material," you grasp hold of it; when you hear the term "spiritual," you grasp hold of that, too. You are continually deceived by the magic of terminology; you never touch the substance of the fact.

Every fact is alive; each has its own inner life respectively. But, in our daily life, the fact appears wearing clothing; that is, it seldom shows itself before us in its naked state. The clothing of facts is "terminology." Terms stand for concepts, and concepts are far from the inner life of facts. We speak of "spirit" or "matter," and by the mere use of these terms we think we have understood matter or spirit. It seems to me, however, that what we call our understanding is nothing but a mechanical handling of these conceptions according to traditional usage, unconscious though we may be of this. It is like gathering up and handing down clothing when the man who wore it is no longer there. The true man can never be known by making use of his former clothing. The inner life of a fact can never be caught by mere intellectual treatment.

A Dialogue Between One and Zero

One: Can we see the inner life too?

Zero: Certainly. But first we must throw off every kind of garment, must free ourselves from the influence of concepts and terminology.

Look! Here on my desk is a white rose in a vase. You see it as white, don't you? Now you must see the flower that is not white, and see the flower that is not a flower, too. It is from here that the inner life of the flower will begin to reveal itself to you.

One: Do tell me more, please!

Zero: You are now observing the white rose. You and the flower are a certain distance apart. You observe the flower; the flower is observed by you. But reverse the point of view to that of the flower. The flower does not know that it is called a white rose. The flower knows no name, no color, no time, no space. The real life of the flower simply goes on within its own unknown mystery. Even the term "mystery" is not adequate to convey what its real inner life is. Listen, here is a story:

The monk Chosei once questioned Master Rei-un:

Chosei: When there is chaos and undifferentiation, what then?

Rei-un: A naked pillar has conceived.

Chosei: When there is differentiation, what then?

Rei-un: It is like a wisp of cloud appearing in the ultimate transparency.

Chosei: I wonder if the ultimate transparency can yield a wisp of cloud or not?

Rei-un did not answer.

Chosei: If so, then anything that has life cannot be there.

Again Rei-un did not answer.

Chosei: The instant that the purest transparency is without a single speck in it, what then?

Rei-un: The ultimate reality still ever renews its flowing.

Chosei: What do you mean by "the ultimate reality ever renews its flowing"?

Rei-un: It is just like the everlasting clarity of a mirror.

Chosei: Then, on the path to enlightenment, is there anything to do?

Rei-un: There is.

Chosei: What is there to do on the path to enlightenment?

Rei-un: Break the mirror, then you and I shall see.

Chosei: When there is chaos and undifferentiation, what kind of beings appear?

Rei-un: It is as if a naked pillar has conceived.

One: You have spoken about the inner life of the flower and told me an interesting dialogue. But I do not understand the relationship between the two.

Zero: Remember that "rose" is merely the name we give to an unfathomable substance according to our conceptual usage. From the beginning of the universe, however, the inner life of that which we name "rose" has not been conscious of its name. It is clear that any kind of name is nothing but a sign attached from outside by some accident to a material substance of fact. The name and the substance, therefore, are definitely unrelated to one another. The name is a differentiating insignia which assumes the role to bring willy-nilly into the spotlight of the intellect something anonymous that has been dwelling in chaos. But the actor's role always ends in failure; for, whenever that which is anonymous is brought into the light of intellection, its original nature or substance is metamorphosed and takes on a quite different character.

One: Then what you call the real life or the inner life is something akin to "chaos" or "the undifferentiated"?

Zero: That is what I would say.

One: How can I see the real life?

Zero: The only way is to grasp it directly from the inside, without any medium.

One: How can I get inside it?

Zero: Here, right now, you are, aren't you?

One: . . . .

Zero: You don't know where you are, even when you are in the midst of the fact. This is because unfortunately you yourself are always repudiating the fact.

One: What can I do about it?

Zero: To put yourself into it, you must first of all see your own real self, which is no other than the true dweller in the chaos. I urge upon you the necessity of discovering your own real self. This

72

is enlightenment. You, however, are not truly aware of your real self, so you cannot see that there is no question but that you are in the midst of reality now.

One: May I ask you about the real self?

Zero: Oh yes, you may ask about it as much as you like. And you may know a great deal about it, too. But though your parent may tell you how you have been brought up since your birth, or a philosopher explain to you endlessly about the existence of the self by means of abstract reasoning—epistemologically, ontologically, ethically, physically, sexually, socially—yet you will grasp nothing of your real self.

One: According to what you say, it would seem that the self is, so to speak, twofold. Is that so?

Zero: In a certain sense that is true. Buddhist philosophy tells us that man must return to his own real self, namely to non-ego. He must awaken to the fact that the self he normally considers to be his self or ego is a false self, full of ignorance and subject to suffering. He must get rid of his false self and see his real self. This real self is the Buddha-nature within every man.

From my own point of view I might state this as follows. We have our daily life in this visible world in which all things exist in a necessary relativity. This mutual relativity is, after all, ego-centered. The visible world in which we live might be called an ego-centered system. In the network of this ego-centered system everything is named and each name designates an individual ego. You were named "One" by your parent. Under this name you were a student; your school teacher distinguished you from the others as a clever boy. Under your name you got a job in an office; you worked day after day and attained a certain position in society, where you wake up, eat, sleep, talk, love, hate, compete, suffer, desire, dream, become old and die. When that time comes your name will be put on a tombstone, though you yourself will already not be there.

There is, however, another system which might refer to the real self, that is, the non-ego-centered system. Within this non-ego-centered system you are not you, the flower is not a flower, the persimmon is not a persimmon, time is not time, space is not space, life is not life, death is not death, love is not love, hate is not hate, competition is not competition, suffering, desire, good, bad, all different kinds of existences, all forms and non-forms, are not themselves. There is only chaos, the undifferentiated fact that "ever renews its flowing."

You noticed that you seem to be a "twofold" you, as you spoke of it. The "you" who has a name may be taken as the *rūpa* self. *Rūpa* means "form" in Buddhist philosophy. And the "you" who dwells in the undifferentiated may be taken as the *sūnyatā* self. *Sūnyatā* generally means "emptiness," but in my view the word emptiness is apt to be thought of as "endless void." Therefore one must see emptiness as Suchness, as "As-it-is-ness." As long as you never step into the midst of un-differentiation, the *sūnyatā* self and the *rūpa* self continue to remain at a distance from one another, separate and unrelated. When, however, by your own effort you break the mirror, you will realize your twofold self to be one actual body. This is the real self. Do you understand?

One: Oh please, let me see it directly! I am really eager to see my real self.

Zero: Hey, One!

One: Yes, sir.

Zero: Hey, One!

One: Yes, sir.

Zero: Hey, One!

One: Yes, sir.

Zero: You blockhead! Where are you?

THE HYMN
OF THE PEARL

Introduction

Deeply embedded in the lore of every culture is the theme of the hero who sets out on a quest, encounters dangers of every kind and at last brings home a treasure. The idea that there is something precious to be found, something that man essentially needs and which itself reciprocally needs to be recovered, is as old as man himself. There is no tradition, no religion, that has not fished for it in the cauldron of myth and molded it to its purposes. The Sumerians used it in Gilgamesh, you can find it in the pages of the Hindu Mahābharata *and endlessly repeated among the ancient Greeks and Norsemen. It is not surprising, therefore, to come upon it in the Gnostic canon, in the Apocryphal Acts of the Apostle Thomas. Sometimes entitled the "Hymn of the Robe of Glory," sometimes the "Hymn of the Soul," and again the "Song of the Apostle Judas Thomas in the Land of the Indians," it is here more accurately called the "Hymn of the Pearl," for it is the Biblical pearl of great price that the hero is sent to retrieve. And where is this treasure to be found? Where else but in the domain of the serpent, the world-encircling Ouroboros that dwells in the waters of darkness.*

So he sets forth, the Prince of the East, leaving father, mother and elder brother, in one sense provisioned for the journey but in another naked. For they strip him of his "robe of glory," while promising that he shall have it back when he has achieved the quest. This gesture is essential to the story. Hero or savior, whichever he be—and here in the Hymn he is,

75

perhaps, both—must go to his tryst defenseless. To be equipped against danger would be to prevent danger from fostering the rescuing power.

Forth he goes into Egypt, settles himself beside the serpent, puts on the garments of the Egyptians and tastes their food and drink. This, of course, as it was with Persephone in Hades, is his undoing, but the myth, for his very herohood, requires that he be undone. So, having eaten, he falls asleep, forgets the Pearl and no longer recognizes himself as a son of the King of the East. But as in the fairy tales, where the dwarf, the frog or the little old woman come to the prince's assistance, so in myth do divine powers come to the aid of the hero. A letter, sent from another level, that of father, mother and brother, flies to him in the form of an eagle, which when it meets him, becomes speech. He wakes and remembers who he is and in doing so remembers the Pearl. Now, with the spell of his father's name, he, in turn, puts the serpent to sleep, seizes the necessary treasure, throws off the garments of the Egyptians and retraces his steps toward his homeland. At this point, because he has found the Pearl, his robe of glory comes to meet him and he hastens to receive it. Thus clothed, and bringing with him his finding, he can return to his father's kingdom, renewed—one could even say reborn—and the fateful quest achieved.

So the hymn is sung and the story ended. But for us the end becomes a beginning. For, faced with this fundamental theme, we ponder on its meaning and search for it in ourselves. Who is the hero? From whence does he come? What does Egypt signify; what the serpent; what the Pearl? Are we being told that a son of Heaven, putting off his starry accoutrements, descends into the world of matter and retrieves from uncomprehending darkness the fallen seed of light? Or is the Pearl rather the lapsed soul that the celestials need to reclaim?

These are questions, not assertions. Symbols, by their nature, are multisided; they cast their light in all directions and are capable of endless interpretations. Anyone reading the Hymn of the Pearl will find his own meaning in it. And it may be that light will be thrown on the story by its Biblical redaction in the parable of the Prodigal Son. He, too, went away from his father's house, descended into his own kind of Egypt and there symbolically fell asleep. But at length, he, too, like the hero of the Pearl,

The Hymn of the Pearl

awoke. *"He came to himself,"* St. Luke tells us, and by means of that recovered self, bearing it with him as a treasure, he arose and returned to his father.

Thus, in one way or another, in hymn, parable, fairy tale, myth, the theme of search repeats itself. Setting out and coming home—these are the heart of the matter. Without the first the second is not possible. The quest is not merely a personal but a cosmic process. The hero, in discovering himself, renews the general life—of man and of the world.

P. L. Travers

When I was a little child
And dwelt in the kingdom of my Father's house,
Resting in the wealth and splendor of those who raised me,
My parents sent me forth from the East, our homeland,
With provisions for the journey.
From the riches of our treasure-house
They tied me a burden.
Great it was, yet light,
So that I might carry it alone. . . .
They took off from me the robe of glory
Which in their love they had made for me,
And my purple mantle that was woven
To conform exactly to my figure,
And made a covenant with me,
And wrote it in my heart
That I might not forget it:

> "When thou goest down into Egypt
> And bringest the one Pearl
> Which lies in the middle of the sea
> Guarded by the devouring serpent,
> Thou shalt put on again thy robe of glory

Triangle

And thy mantle over it
And with thy brother, our next in rank,
Be heir in our kingdom."

I left the East
And journeyed downward with two guides,
For the way was dangerous and difficult
And I was untried in traveling it.
I passed over the borders of Maishan,
The gathering-place of the merchants of the East,
And came into the land of Babel
And entered within the walls of Sarbug.
I went down into Egypt
And my companions took their leave of me.

By the quickest way, I set forth to the serpent
And settled close by his dwelling place,
Watching for him to slumber and sleep
So that I might take the Pearl from him.
I was alone and a stranger there
Until I saw a kinsman from the East,
A fair, well-favored youth, and son of kings.
He came and attached himself to me
And I made him a friend and partaker in my quest.
I warned him against the Egyptians
And against consorting with the unclean.
But I clothed myself in their garments
Lest I should seem as one that had come from without
To recover the Pearl,
And lest the Egyptians should arouse the serpent against me.
Yet in some way or other
They perceived that I was not their countryman.

صورة النسر على ما يرى في السما

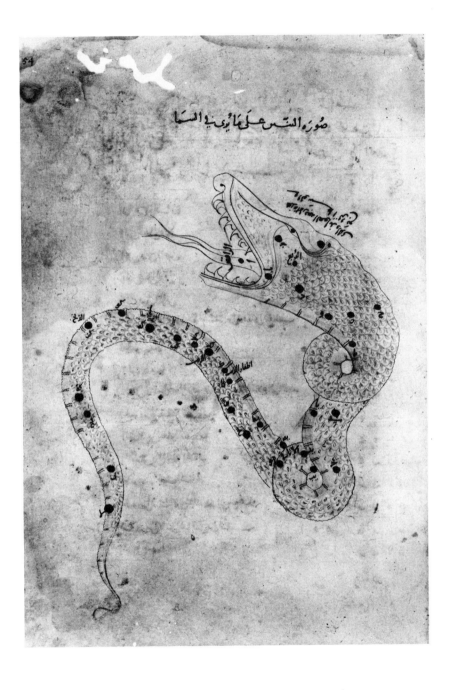

Triangle

They ingratiated themselves with me,
And mixed me drink with their cunning
And gave me to taste of their meat.
I forgot that I was a king's son
And served their king.
I forgot the Pearl
For which my parents had sent me.
Through the heaviness of their nourishment
I sank into deep slumber.

All this that befell me,
My parents marked,
And they grieved for me.
It was proclaimed in our kingdom
That all should come to our gates.
And the kings and princes of Parthia
And all the nobles of the East
Wove a plan that I must not be left in Egypt.
And they wrote a letter to me
And each of the great ones signed it with his name:

> "From thy Father, the King of kings, and from thy mother, mistress of the East, and from thy brother, our next in rank, unto thee, our son in Egypt, peace.
> "Awake, and rise up out of thy sleep, and perceive the words of our letter. Remember that thou art a king's son: behold whom thou hast served in bondage. Be mindful of the Pearl, for whose sake thou hast departed into Egypt. Remember thy robe of glory, recall thy splendid mantle, that thou mayest put them on and deck thyself with them, and that thy name be read in the book of heroes, and thou become with thy brother, our deputy, heir in our kingdom."

The Hymn of the Pearl

Like a messenger was the letter
That the King had sealed with his right hand.
It rose up in the form of an eagle,
The king of all birds,
And flew until it alighted beside me
And became wholly speech.
At its voice and sound I awoke
And arose from my sleep.
The words of the letter
Were as the words of my heart.
I remembered that I was a king's son,
And my freeborn soul longed for its kind.
I remembered the Pearl
For which I had been sent down to Egypt,
And I began to enchant
The terrible and devouring serpent.
I overcame him by naming
The name of my Father upon him,
The name of our next in rank,
And the name of my mother, the queen of the East.
I seized the Pearl,
And turned to go back to my Father's house.
Their filthy garment I shed,
And left it behind in the land of Egypt,
And directed my way that I might come
To the light of our homeland, the East.
The letter which had awakened me
I found before me on the way.
As it had awakened me with its voice,
So it guided me with its light
That glowed before me.
With its voice it encouraged me,
And with its love it drew me on. . . .

Triangle

My robe of glory which I had put off
And my mantle that went over it
From our home on high
Had my parents sent to greet me
By the hands of their faithful treasurers.
Its splendor I had forgotten,
For in my childhood
I had left it in my Father's house.
As I now beheld the robe
It seemed suddenly to become
Like a mirror of myself.
Myself entire I saw in it,
And it entire I saw in myself,
That we were two in separateness,
And yet again one
In the sameness of our forms.
The image of the King of kings
Was all in all of it.
And I saw that through it, the movements of knowledge
Were being sent forth. . . .
Yearning arose in me
To run toward it and receive it.
And I stretched toward it and took it
And decked myself with the beauty of its colors.
I cast the royal mantle
About my entire self.

Clothed therein, I ascended
To the gate of salutation and adoration.
I bowed my head
And adored the splendor of my Father
Who had sent it to me,
Whose commands I had fulfilled
As he too had done that which he promised.

The Cosmos.

Triangle

At the gates of his kingdom,
Which was from the beginning,
He received me joyfully.
And all his servants praised him with organ voice
For his promise that I should journey
From the court of the King of kings
And having found my Pearl
Should appear together with him.

THE SEARCH FOR A WISE MAN

Jacob Needleman

In the Bibliothèque Nationale in Paris there is an anonymous twelfth-century Hermetic manuscript containing a remarkable illustration of the cosmic scheme as envisioned by Christianity. Like many such diagrams which have come down to us from the prescientific era, it shows a universe created on the principles of conscious emanation and gradations of reality, symbolized by concentric circles with the earth at the center and the Creator enthroned above the highest, outermost sphere. What is unusual about the picture is that unlike most familiar representations of the so-called "geocentric" universe, it has superimposed upon it a number of human figures, each placed at different levels between the person of Christ "above" and the earth "below." Even more striking is that each of these human figures holds his hand outstretched to the one above him.

This diagram can communicate a rather special idea, also shared by all the great spiritual traditions of the past: that the growth of man's being is somehow coordinate with the very structure of the universe, that psychological change, in its deepest and most basic sense, is not merely a subjective process that takes place apart from the laws of nature. On the contrary, it occurs according to objective laws, the same laws by which the world we see, as well as the worlds we cannot see, are born, preserved and destroyed. The evolution of consciousness is both a cosmic fact and a human possibility. Therefore, in a fundamental sense, the development of man's being is meant to follow a "track" already laid down for him in the makeup of reality. Such is the traditional idea.

If we wish to understand the nature of the "wise man," or the "spiritual guide," there is much help to be drawn from this cosmic

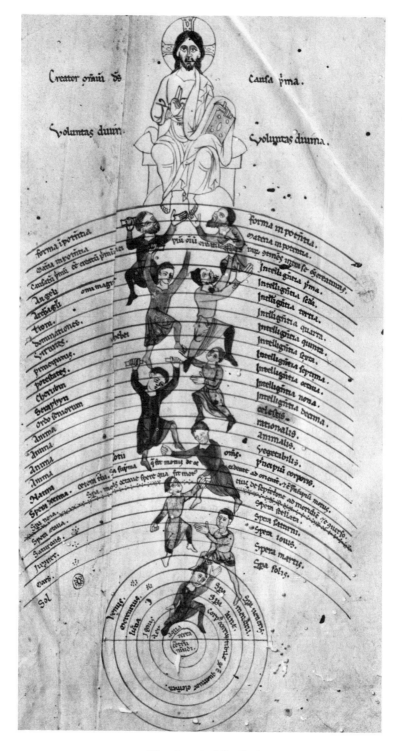

The Ascent of the Soul.

perspective. Let us look more closely at the illustration. Among the figures placed at different levels there are several whose faces are directed not upward, toward Christ, but downward, toward those human beings at the lower levels of ascent. Why? Why are they not directing their attention, like the others, toward the ultimate goal—liberation from the spheres of the "world," and union with God? Surely, this is an indication that not only is there a "track" laid down for the seeker in the very nature of reality, but also that reality contains in its essence a factor of divine care for man. Having said that, however, it is necessary to emphasize that the man to whom this care is directed is he who has already left "earth," whose hand is stretched upward.

What emerges here is a picture of *a sacred universe*. One has only to enter a Gothic cathedral to understand something of what is being depicted in the illustration. The medieval cathedral was nothing less than a model of the universe. What we appreciate as the "beauty" of the cathedral was the representation of that element in reality which can attract the human heart toward God. The cathedral, the universe, is fundamentally a place in which man is to seek God and in which God is able to be sought. This cathedral, this model of the universe, was built on the basis of a renewed discovery of the interrelationship between the symbolism of geometry and the teachings of religion. The true dynamism of the cosmos is "visible" only to the man who is in the act of reaching upward. This dynamism has to do with the deep interrelationship between universal laws of nature and the transformation of being. Cosmic care for man lies at the heart of reality; but to be cared for, man must seek.

And thus our attention comes to rest on what is for us the most significant aspect of the illustration. One figure is not only looking downward, but has also grasped the outstretched hand of the man beneath him. This relationship does not occur at the upper levels of progression, nor does it obtain at the very lowest stages. It occurs not quite halfway up through the "spheres."

One is tempted to think of this particular figure as the paradigm of the spiritual teacher, although all the relationships in the diagrams need to be considered. Nevertheless, it is apparent that the care of man which is coordinate with the structure of the cosmos is not to be understood too quickly as some general force, some general arrangement of the elements of reality. Something rather more specific seems to be depicted: namely, that cosmic care for man (who seeks) exists in the form of guidance and help through the instrumentality of other human beings.

It should be pointed out that we might have gone to any number of traditional sources for this idea, once we have discovered how to look for it. In the traditions of Asia the spiritual guide is understood to be an incarnation on earth of the supreme metaphysical reality. And his relationship to his disciples reflects in miniature the manner in which the Absolute creates, destroys, maintains and reabsorbs into itself the whole of the universal order. "Guru is Brahman" (the Absolute) is too hastily interpreted by many Westerners as either a preposterous overestimation of the spiritual guide or else as a "figure of speech." It is truer to the traditional meaning of this formula to approach it from the direction we are discovering in our Hermetic/Christian illustration. Brahman *teaches.* Not, of course, through merely verbal formulations, but by an ontological process which obeys specific universal laws, having to do with the origination and development of energies.

In Mahayana Buddhism, the Buddha (the Awakened) is also understood as the manifestation, in the world of relative reality, of the supreme Truth-of-Being (Emptiness). This doctrine developed in Tibetan tradition the concept of *tulku,* the incarnated lama who is a manifestation of a universal principle for the sake of all creatures living in the world of illusion. The same general teaching is in Judaism as well. In *The Zohar,* the principal text of the Kabbalah, we find the wise man described as the very "life of the universe."

But what are all these traditions saying today to a man in search of himself? Specifically, they are telling us that the "wise man" and his actions, his teaching, have to be approached in terms of *events at the level of being,* and not simply as *events at the level of psyche.*

The distinction between psyche and being is the distinction between what I feel, what I desire, what I believe, think, perceive, sense and imagine—and whether *I am,* whether *I* exist at all. A man who is psychologically great may be ontologically ordinary. To appreciate this is to recognize an exceedingly important corollary: if the spiritual guide and his teaching concern events at the level of being, then we must also say that the search for a teacher must also be an event at the level of being

88

A Vardapet (Wise Man) Isaiah Teaching.

and not merely or solely an event at the level of psyche.

Such ideas put into question the quality of modern man's own search, no matter how "intense" and "sincere" it seems to be. At the same time, a deeper kind of hope is to be found in this perspective, a hope that links authentic search to the universe itself.

In the contemporary era, the first glimpse of the cosmic nature of the spiritual process came with the introduction into the West of the teachings of Zen Buddhism. In the accounts offered by D. T. Suzuki of the transactions between Zen master and pupil, one began to feel the great scale of this process. The teacher was seeking to create in the pupil an experience on the level of being. The mystery of *being*, like every great mystery of the eternal teachings, is not simply an intellectual puzzle, nor even necessarily a problem to be solved. In the Zen tradition, this experience has to do with something "beyond words," "beyond the intellect," "not explainable by reason," "irrational."

It began to be understood that through a teacher one may discover the experience of a search for oneself as a search for *being*. This placed the transaction between Zen master and pupil on a completely different scale from the familiar conception of the transactions between priest and believer, educator and student, psychiatrist and patient.

In effect, the master was—to return for a moment to our cosmic diagram—pulling up the pupil by his hair.

There was no question here of beginning the search for a teacher rightly or wrongly. No need to worry about the right criteria for a teacher, no need to concern oneself about his "credentials." For how *could* a search begin "rightly"? One is a beginner, one "knows" a great deal and understands nothing; what in oneself can be trusted to see rightly the qualities of this or that man? The main thing was—to approach a teacher!

The problem of selecting the right teacher, or of finding an authentic teacher—problems which figure so largely in the contemporary eclectic "spiritual" situation—never seemed to arise in this body of literature. The literature of Zen provides a special meaning to the idea of the spiritual teacher's "credentials." Like every tradition, Zen maintains a rigorous rule of transmission by which "the role of the master" is handed down to a successor. But it is *only in the encounter* between the

Taikan

Lao-Tzu and a Sleeping Pupil.

teacher and pupil that the meaning of these "credentials" is understood.

The sacred books of the East are replete with treatises enumerating the qualities which an authentic teacher must possess. He must be compassionate, must have perfect knowledge of the teaching, he must be "God-realized"—the list can be very long indeed. But what is a person who has not yet entered an authentic path to make of these qualities? What we ordinarily understand as "compassion" or "knowledge" may have no useful relationship to what such terms mean within the action of the tradition itself.

There is a Zen story which very well illustrates what is entailed in approaching and "testing" the master.

A famous samurai warrior once entered the chambers of a Zen master, saying: "I have heard that you know the secret of heaven and hell. Please instruct me!"

The teacher looked up at the warrior, bedecked in his magnificent armor, his head held high. "Who are you?" the master asked, without much interest.

"I am a *samurai!*"

The master laughed. "You? You are a samurai? Don't make me spew!"

At this, the great warrior's face darkened; he drew his gleaming sword and lunged forward to bring it down upon the master's head.

"There open the gates of hell," the master remarked, looking directly into the warrior's eyes.

The samurai froze, his sword arrested in midair. In a moment of intense self-seeing, with all his pride and egoism nakedly revealed to him, he silently bowed his head and slowly replaced his sword. He stood there, head down, not moving.

Quietly, the master added: "And here open the gates of heaven."

One can regard this story as a lesson concerning the inner event which a teacher calls forth. Did the warrior have a preconceived idea of what it meant to learn, or what kind of knowledge a spiritual master possesses? All that is washed away in the moment he sees his own weakness. The event on the level of being is not his anger before he sees; it is not even his shame, which is only a reaction to what he has seen. The real event is the seeing itself. Everything else only exists on the level of psyche, that is, it is under the sway of thought-associations, images of self and world, which are little more than fantasies, but which have captured all the real energy of presence within the man.

The stories of the Zen tradition almost always concern the release of this mysterious energy of the self. The recognition of this pure energy by the ego produces a shock, often joyous, in which the "I" that has been suffering for so long to affirm its being suddenly recognizes what its source and real being is.

In the Hindu tradition, notably in the *Bhagavad Gītā*, the cosmic symbolism of the path of transformation is so strongly expressed that even a modern reader senses the exalted nature of man's possible movement toward being. The difficulty of entering into this movement of the transformation of being is specifically described in terms of the encounter between the seeker, the warrior Arjuna, and the guru, Krishna, God-Who-Teaches.

Such Hindu texts, like those of many traditions, use mythic language. Unlike discursively formulated dogmas, where mystery is relegated to what simply cannot be understood, mythic language exerts extraordinary pressure on man through a predetermined double impact: it cannot be understood, but at the same time it must be understood. Myth has its three-dimensional analogue in the pressure placed upon a pupil in the presence of the master. The pupil cannot understand, but must understand.

Hindu tradition indicates that to be a pupil is as demanding as the cosmos is great. The great warrior Arjuna himself struggles against the demand that Krishna places upon him in the very first chapter of the *Bhagavad Gītā.*

What it entails to be an authentic pupil is tellingly illustrated in the fifteenth-century Hindu treatise, the *Vedāntasāra* ("The Essence of the Doctrines of Vedānta"), summarized by Heinrich Zimmer in *The Philosophies of India.* The list of requirements which the potential pupil must satisfy is truly awesome, being in every respect comparable to the equally awesome criteria which are established for the authentic teacher.

Just as the teacher must be "perfect" in his knowledge, so the pupil must be "perfect" in his wish for knowledge.

Just as a man carrying on his head a load of wood that has caught fire would go rushing to a pond to quench the flames, even so should the adhikarin *[the "competent student"], scorched with the mad pains of the fire of life in the world, its birth, its death, its self-deluding futility, go rushing to a guru learned in the Vedas, who, himself having reached the goal of Vedānta, now abides serene in uninterrupted consciousness of the essence of imperishable beings. The* adhikarin *is to come to this guru bearing presents in his hand, ready to serve, and prepared to obey in every way.*

The treatise goes on to list an astonishing array of powers and virtues which appear to be attributes of one already far along the path. For example, the pupil must have an attitude that "keeps the mind from being troubled by sense objects—the only sense activity permitted to the student . . . being that of listening eagerly to the words of his guru." The student must have made "a decisive turning away" from "the entire system of the outer world." He must have "the power to endure without the slightest discomposure extremes of heat and cold, weal and woe, honor and abuse, loss and gain."

It is necessary, of course, to find the principle behind these formulations. When taken too literally, they would place the possible encounter with a teacher out of reach of most modern people, who, far from having intentionally worked to the limits of any traditional orthodoxy, have not even been automatically prepared through the absorption of the values and impressions provided by a traditional cultural environment.

Concerning this principle, it is perhaps most important to recognize one rather clear fact about what we are calling a "traditional cultural environment." Such an environment is one in which, to some extent, the teachings are already reaching out to people. Here we do not refer to those "clearly marked channels," discussed above in connection with a tradition such as Zen, where anyone who is sufficiently interested can discover one or another form of intensive spiritual practice. We mean something far broader and less defined—the moral values, the fundamental principles and ideas, the social forms and institutions, the art, the literature, the habits and customs, most of which trace their origin, albeit often tortuously and in diluted fashion, to a central body of spiritual teachings.

What, then, is the principle we are seeking to discern? What actually is "high" about beginning on the path or recognizing the teacher? To answer that we have to ask more insistently about what it means that a teaching "reaches out" to man. How does it do this? And how could it do this today in an environment that has almost completely destroyed or replaced all the remnants of its own traditional core? Does what we are calling the "event on the level of being" depend so much on the cultural milieu? Or is it rather that for a teaching to be a living teaching and not solely a glorious but ineffective fossil, it must reach us where we actually are and somehow make it possible for the *question*, the ontological event, to take place even in the depths of hell?

Can an authentic teacher appear and make it possible for modern man to recognize him? Who can "pull us up by our hair"?

We have reached the heart of our subject.

I have been trying to allow the traditional texts themselves to speak about one fundamental element in the relationship between teacher and pupil. I hope that something has come through concerning the mystery of the change of inner being which is offered man on the spiritual path.

A fuller treatment of this theme would have brought out many more aspects of our Christian/Hermetic diagram—for example, the astonishing notion that every creature beneath the level of God himself is a pupil of the higher. And this would have required us to consider as fully as possible the ancient idea that real human learning involves an exchange of energies and an interaction of forces identical in nature to the movement of forces by which the universe itself comes into being.

To do justice to the idea that man on the path is actually "higher man," we might have gone to the legends and myths of the Teutons dealing with the struggles of the gods, which symbolize the effort toward spiritual liberation of men with greater understanding and being. Or we might have cited the traditions of ancient and medieval Iran, so profoundly illuminated by Henry Corbin, where it is said that only a man who possesses a "soul," the "body of light" (a "subtle organism independent of his material organism"), can meet with and become the pupil of the spiritual guide.

But we must now try to speak directly to the problem facing contemporary man in search of a guide. How does it stand, then, with the modern person "in search of a wise man"? The following is a phenomenological portrait which has been put together from direct observation of a large number of people, young and old, representing many walks of life. Included are also elements drawn from my own personal experience.

We must give our seeker a definite background of conventional religious experience. He has, at least once in his life, entered a church or synagogue in a condition of need. Let us say that he has gone directly to the priest as well. He has laid his suffering before the altar of religion, in its modern, Western form.

Having entered in a condition of need, he has come away with a strengthened religious personality. He has been given energy to face the doubt in himself and overcome it, to face the fear in himself and resist it; he takes arms against certain desires; a sense of belonging (whether to God or to the community) bolsters him against the emotions of self-pity and loneliness; a tincture of theology calms his restless intellect.

Having the strength now to face life, the future seeker soon runs head on into the worlds around him, the worlds of success and failure, love and betrayal, newspapers, television and cinema, books and art, war and human injustice. He discovers that he has a political personality, a scientific personality, an artistic personality, a sexual personality, a vacation personality, and so on.

Thrown by life from one world into another, from one personality into another, he begins to sense the question, "Who am I?" and reaches the conclusion that he does not know.

He sees and yet does not see that this question is the most intimate aspect of his being. Everything in the life around him is urging him to make a choice, to define himself. But each attempt succeeds only for a while, until another of his personalities is activated. Again and again, the question arises in him—not simply, what shall I do? where shall I go? but rather: who, what, is the being which calls itself by my name?

Turning again to religion, he finds—he does not know why—that it no longer helps. He blames himself and not religion, but the fact is that when again the intimate question, "Who am I?" surges up in him he finds religion as but one item on the menu. It too, wants to "solve," that is to say, destroy, his question.

Is there something wrong with him? He considers psychotherapy and perhaps tries it for a while.

But it is too late for psychotherapy—because he has already begun
to read certain books containing ideas that make a new demand upon
him, and in the light of which he is not so torn between the dualism
of his own question and the many answers offered by the multitude of
personalities within him. He is interested to discover that he has a rather
definite sense of discrimination among all these mystical, Oriental and
esoteric books which he now finds everywhere he goes.

Standing alone in front of a rack of texts dealing with the whole
range of "the spiritual explosion," he finds in himself surprisingly little
indecision or difficulty selecting the books he wants to read. Why is
this? How is it that this man who in every other aspect of his life is
hurled from one world to another, who can take no stand even in the
details of his life, here finds that he knows what he wants?

Of course, very little is as yet actually at stake. It is only a book, only
a few dollars. But were he to reflect upon himself he might recognize
that something purer is operating in him. He might feel, probably un-
consciously, that a certain dream, going far back to his childhood, is now
being aroused and nourished. It is the dream of the wise man, the dream
of Great Learning. And it is connected, in a way he does not understand,
with the intimate question of his being.

But now a more problematic stage is reached. He begins to be seri-
ously interested in the fact that all around him are followers of
"spiritual paths." He goes to lectures, begins to ask questions. He meets
people who are known as teachers, gurus or spiritual guides.

He must choose, not only among teachers, but from among tradi-
tions, from among whole universes bearing the weight of history and
culture not his own; or, if in some sense his own, containing ideas which
he can hardly understand, far less accept as true.

Shall he respond to the man or his ideas? Shall he trust his feeling
or his thought? He liked that teacher—is that a right basis? He was made
uncomfortable by the other—perhaps that is a truer help. Here stands
a recognized master, authorized, bearing the "robe of the lineage"—
surely one must give that serious weight; that other comes from God
knows where, has put together something exciting, but what is it? Can
he trust his life to it?

In short, he has found the worlds-upon-worlds have followed him

Bernard Leach

The Pilgrim.

into the spiritual search. He is tossed from one to the other—and this is so even if he chooses to follow this or that leader; in six months, or a year, or five, with whom will he be then? And why? How long to stay, when to give up and try another? Perhaps give up everything and accept life as it is?

But now he has found—because of all this—something exceedingly important, exceedingly subtle and interesting. His question, the question of his being, has not let go of him; it has dogged him into the very pockets of the gods; it is not as fragile as he thought. He knows it is acting upon him; now and then, all too infrequently and lasting perhaps but a moment, it breaks in upon him and gives him the strength to wait, to not choose, to be cautious outwardly because inwardly something very daring is possible: to be silent and alert, ready without tension to move when it is right to move.

difficult
Stage 0

The problems of his life now assume a different place. They continue to overwhelm him, to take all his attention, but more and more a thought appears that is energized by what he has seen of himself and suffered of himself. His question is now seeking to break through more and more—perhaps it happens in his dreams, what were once called "sacred dreams," the dreams that awaken a man from sleep rather than protect his sleep as do the dreams of fallen-away man.

And it is here that we who are pondering the question of the search for the wise man must stop and reflect upon the harmony of psyche and cosmos that our Hermetic diagram depicts. What force, beyond psychology, is moving in this man, who, let us hope, is also ourselves? Where does it come from and toward what great unity, unknown under the names of happiness and satisfaction, is it driving? And if this is a universe of conscious law, drawing all beings upward who seek to be drawn, and even those, in the end, who do not seek, but only wish to seek—if this is such a universe, and if our earth is part of that universe, how can I not imagine that all around are helping powers waiting for me to raise my hand blindly up, to raise up my own question which comes not from the psyche, but from the subtle and fleeting and merciful destruction of my psyche?

It is said, "When the pupil is ready, the teacher appears." How could we now think of this as anything but a cosmic law, which means that no outer conditions arranged by human history can stand in its way?

Am I ?

I wonder about the aspect of tenderness

Triangle

Yet obviously, man—I myself—can stand in its way.

Let us conclude by considering that all the wise men or teachers now in our midst are authentic—forgetting for a moment that there are such things as frauds, charlatans, impostors. Forget also the notion of a teaching or teacher suited to my particular needs, or the needs of this era. Consider only that the intelligence and spiritual instinct I need is given by my question, it is not something I can develop or improve upon by my own efforts. Now, here, pondering what to do, how to seek, whom to choose, I make my move and see that in that movement, that impulse of reaching out, I have lost my own question, I am no longer in the center of the question of my being.

But seeing that, accepting that I am lost again in the illusions of decision, my question instantly returns. Then, and only then, can I silently ask for a guide; and then, and only then, so it is said, is Reality obliged to yield the guide up to me.

MEETINGS WITH REMARKABLE MEN

One Man's Search Becomes a Film

P. L. Travers

After completing his vast cosmological allegory, *All and Everything,*
George Ivanovitch Gurdjieff set to work on his autobiographical *Meetings
with Remarkable Men* with the energy—both as man and teacher—of the
heroes of myth or such historical figures as Marpa the Translator. The
"Second Series," as this personal story came to be called by the author,
is clearly designed to throw light on the universal concepts of the first
book and to give them, as it were, a local habitation and an understand-
able name. But here, too, there are underlying elements of allegory and
fable, multiple levels of meaning and continually repeated themes such
as one finds in Rūmī, Attār and other fabulous Eastern writers. Gurdjieff
was, in fact, a natural storyteller in the orotund, flamboyant, many-
faceted tradition of the Orient; and at the very outset he establishes the
reader in a part of the world where Sinbad the Sailor traditionally casts
anchor and the story of Moses, told in bazaars, can still make the hearer
catch his breath.

Some element, perhaps, came to him from his father who, in his
time, was a celebrated bard—or *ashokh*—in Armenia. A child who has
been fed on patriarchal folklore and lulled to sleep with the story of
Gilgamesh will always bear their traces in him, a rich inheritance. But
the impulse of the storyteller comes essentially from the desire to com-
municate—it is not necessarily handed down—and the true mark of the
storyteller is his delight in the telling. These were Gurdjieff's own, and
in *Meetings with Remarkable Men* they play their lights over a world far

enough away from us to seem, for all the factual detail, as mythical as Atlantis. This little company of remarkable men, calling themselves "The Seekers of Truth" and following their elusive goal through the remotest parts of Asia, have names, birthdates, cards of identity; in any ordinary biography they would pass for what they, in fact, were—ordinary men pursuing the professions of doctor, scientist, engineer. It is not merely the author's affection for them—tenderness for friends is a strong element in the book—that builds them into hero size. What turns them into Argonauts is the nature of their search; that, and the storyteller's awareness that to speak of what cannot be told is only possible by implication and allusion, by giving the thing, in fact, an air of parable. In this way it is made clear that in essence every one of these characters, not least the author himself, is sib to Gilgamesh.

It will surprise nobody that such a book, with its heroic figures, its turbulent inner and outer adventures, its humor and its mystical overtones, should have been made into a film. Written and directed by Peter Brook together with Gurdjieff's closest pupil, Madame Jeanne de Salzmann, the scenario, for all its mythical quality, has, since it closely follows the text, an air of authenticity. This extraordinary caravan, drawn in the wake of Gurdjieff's own unflagging thirst for truth, is composed of actual, if motley, human beings. How he collected them, or by the mystery of coincidence came upon them, is an essential part of the story. He was the instrument, the catalyst, by means of which the search itself drew them all together.

In the film, as in the book, we first see him as a child, in close companionship with his father, the patriarchal bard, and his tutor, the dean of Kars Cathedral. These two friends who, in Gurdjieff's words, "had taken upon themselves the obligation of preparing me for responsible life," had the habit, commonly found in Eastern cultures, of communicating with each other by means of spontaneous question and answer.

> "For instance, one evening when I was in the workshop, my future tutor entered unexpectedly and asked my father, 'Where is God just now?'
>
> "My father answered most seriously, 'God is just now in Sarika-mis.'

Ashokhs *in the film "Meetings with Remarkable Men"*

" 'What is God doing there?'

" 'He is making double ladders and on the tops of them he is fastening happiness, so that individual people and whole nations might ascend and descend.' "

The listening boy absorbs it all, and from the outset it is made clear in the film that with such preceptors as this, his will be no ordinary childhood; that these two will foster his destiny and engender the arising in him of questions that need to be answered.

Indeed, we ourselves, along with the child, are plunged into question in the opening scene. What are we to make of the strange Caucasian mountain valley which has the property of giving back from its rocky slopes certain musical sounds—not all sounds, it must be said, only those made by a musician who, in Gurdjieff's later formulation, arrives at the state of "Self-awareness." One bard after another plays a tune and to one, alone, the rocks reply. Nothing is explained in words. We, with the child, are left wondering and at the same time somehow made aware that the keynote of the story has been struck. We are in the presence of mystery, at once macrocosmic and microcosmic.

It so happens—although it is not to be found in the book itself—that we have a clue to this part of the scenario in a private report of one of Gurdjieff's group meetings which took place in Paris in 1944. In reading it we must bear in mind that Gurdjieff's method of teaching was essentially parabolic. He went roundabout to make his points, never failing to abide by his own injunction—"Always begin from afar"; telling an inconsequent story whose relevance might become apparent only to one pair of ears; murmuring "More red pepper!" to somebody who, far from being involved in culinary activity, was sitting idly in a chair. I have heard him speak a word to one pupil that another would know was meant for himself alone; create laughter at his own end of the table while somebody at the other end, perceiving the intention behind the joke, would turn aside and weep. "Remember," he would often say, "everything has seven aspects." We should take that reminder into account when we confront this report of one of his groups. Let us listen to it.

Paris, January 11, 1944

Mr. G. has given an exercise to a group of pupils.

Afterward, he challenges them by showing an engraving

representing seven Oriental dancers wearing gigantic headdresses surmounted by antennas. Some are striking tambourines, others blowing pipes like flutes, while together they execute various movements under the direction of their leader, who holds in his hand a curious instrument which looks something like a pennant.

Mr. G. asks each pupil to give an opinion as to what this picture represents. All are mystified. Someone thinks it is a Tibetan dance.

Mr. G.: That is it. The scene is in Tibet. I have been there myself and heard the music that these dancers make. One arrives at a valley in the foothills and there one suddenly hears music—not merely of tambourine and flute, but something infinitely more, music such as never was, truly celestial. But where did it come from, I wanted to know. All around there were nothing but mountains, no house to be seen, no human being. What was the cause of this divine harmony? There was music and yet, at the same time, there was no music. You can imagine what an impression it made. Later I was to decipher the secret and to be myself initiated into the ceremony you see in the picture. But at that first encounter—well, you will understand my astonishment, I who had seen so many marvels, but nothing like to this. For two or three days I could not sleep, questioning within myself about this mystery. I had heard music where neither man nor house existed, nothing but snow and mountains. I was overwhelmed, electrified. Only two years later, when I had pondered long upon this phenomenon did I realize what it meant.

Look! You will see that the leader in the picture holds in his hand an apparatus, which has properties akin to what we would nowadays call a radio—this, remember, was thirty-five years ago, long before radios were in general use. With this apparatus, as you see, he directs—not the music, for there is no music—he directs the vibrations that are issuing forth from the special movements of the dancers' bodies; more than that, from the totality of their experiencing. These vibrations are gathered into the globes they are wearing on their heads. And down in the valley there is a second instrument, corresponding to the one held by the leader, which, when contact between the two is established, collects the vibrations made by the dancers and transmits them in the form of music. Even so, as I said, there is no music, no instrument. Is not this a miracle?

"But they have tambourines and flutes!" somebody protests.

Mr. G.: Yes, they help. They are part of the whole phenomenon, but it is not these that make the music of which I speak. That comes from the bodily movements and the inner psychological exercises of the dancers. It is well known that any strong experience can give vibrations and that experiences of a specific inner intensity —such as the dancers in the picture are undergoing—can give vibrations capable of producing music, divine music. One can oneself arrive at such results by means of a certain effort. But there must be a harmony of the general whole, of the totality of a man, otherwise there is discord. A precise inner attitude is necessary in order to produce this celestial music.

Do you realize what it means to arrive at such a point? These dancers must have studied these special movements since childhood and only now, as old men, are they able to participate in the ceremony. Imagine how they have had to work! Compared to their efforts, the exercises you have all done a while ago are nothing but child's play. But this that I have shown you will help you to understand my so often repeated instructions with regard to the intentional motions of the body. For example, do not make a movement with the whole leg when what is required is merely a gesture with the foot. The leg may be needed for some quite different purpose. It is the same with all the limbs. These movements need a very complete attention. Everything must be done correctly from the outset, with exactitude and respect for detail. Perhaps we shall not achieve music. That does not matter. It is not a question of music but of a real experiencing of the I AM. There are seven exercises for this, one of which you have already been given. If with the mind alone you were to repeat "I am" for a thousand years, it would give you nothing real. But this exercise, carried out with fidelity, can help toward the true I AM. Accuracy and exactitude from the very beginning—that is what is necessary. Only this exactitude in our work can give exact results. Remember what I heard in those mountains. One movement inexactly executed by those seven dancers and everything would have been lost. One discordant note and the result would be cacophony. What must be aimed for is the totality of the attention, attention in all one's parts.

Mr. G. dismisses the group.

Meetings with Remarkable Men

And so we are left with a mystery. There is music and yet there is
no music. We must grapple, it seems, with paradox, unless perhaps—
is that the answer?—we become ourselves parabolists and adapt our all
too crystallized minds to the "seven-aspectedness" of things. "It is not
a question of music," says Gurdjieff, "but of a real experiencing of the
I AM." At the same time he brings together mountain, valley, man,
music. Can it be that he is telling us that what we so glibly call the music
of the spheres is nothing other than a cosmic I AM which must of
necessity resound in man if he is consciously to become part of the
cosmos? Was this, indeed, the Golden Fleece, that, however dimly ap-
prehended, led the young seekers onward? One cannot but assume that
this was so, nor doubt that, with such a goal, there will be many
vicissitudes. The events of the story, always larger than life, always
packed with the stuff of myth, lead past many a Scylla and Charybdis.
These must be thought of as both psychological and factual, for clearly
all quests lead inward as well as outward. For instance, the place of
existence of the Brotherhood of Sarmoung, named in the film as the
object of the search, may indeed be a geographical location. On the
other hand, it could be a latitude of the soul. Words may be read on
many levels. The reader is entitled to find in them psychological as well
as factual dimensions. But the medium of film, by necessity, demands
visual representation. Ideas must be given body, thought made palpa-
ble. The landscapes, so accurately described in the book, permeated as
they are with their own mythology, must be depicted with equal accu-
racy in the film.

So the story conveys us, not past a background of painted panora-
mas, but through regions that are packed with history and are all to be
found on the map. However, as they proceed, each great classical terrain
turns a blank face to the seekers. "Not here, not here!" the Sphinx
assures them. "Nor here!" says the Gobi Desert. The clues so far have
failed them. One by one the remarkable men fall away from their leader,
not so much forsaking him as bent on pursuing their particular paths.
Gurdjieff, led by fate—or instinct—goes alone to Bukhara. And there,
in this ancient cosmopolis, where the caravans of the world meet and
exchange their merchandise—silks, spices, legends, dogmas—he hears
the word "Sarmoung" spoken and feels it reverberate within him. "At

the right moment," he is told—how often we have heard the phrase in myth and fairy tale!—"there will be someone to guide you." So—as was inevitable—moment and guide arrive together and lead him blindfold on a formidable journey to a mysterious unknown monastery. Or perhaps one should say to the end of the world—for that is what it seems like. Has he at last discovered Sarmoung? We do not know. We are not told. And we do not need to be told. Posture can speak more loudly than words—the body has its own story to tell—and the stance of the young Gurdjieff, as he watches the caravan of the last and dearest of his fellow-seekers disappear into the mountains, is not the stance of a man defeated but of one full of confidence and expectation. And with this wordless affirmation, the scenario comes to an end.

It is not, however, the end of the story which, if it begins as an exemplary fable—many will think of it as that—terminates in the history books and the corporeal world of fact.

Sarmoung may not, indeed, exist, but there is sufficient authentic data to assure us that Gurdjieff somehow, somewhere, guided by who knows what presences, sought for and found the system of traditional teaching that, as the mythical hero must return with the treasure, he brought back to the world. Ouspensky, his most famous pupil, bears witness, in *In Search of the Miraculous,* to the fact that Gurdjieff was conveying this teaching in Moscow before World War I. Another of his followers, Thomas de Hartmann, the Russian composer, tells how Gurdjieff, with a train of disciples, escaped, enduring terrible hardships, to Constantinople and thence to the West. Various pupils have written books about the "Institute for the Harmonious Development of Man" that he established in the forest of Fontainebleau. Others have vividly described his last abundant years in Paris. The young man who went seeking for truth became the old man who had found it—an old man massive and serene, as ferocious at times as a Zen master, at others full of compassion for his fellows; a teacher using every moment as a moment of instruction; a master dispensing largesse from his plentiful inner store; a coryphaeus initiating special pupils into the sacred dances that at Sarmoung he himself had learned.

"Each teacher," wrote Farīd al-Dīn 'Attār, in the twelfth century, "reveals his ideas in his own special way and then he disappears."

Gurdjieff revealed his ancient themes, which he spoke of as the Great Knowledge, in his own highly idiosyncratic manner. And in 1949 he disappeared—except from the memory of his pupils. To them and to many who never knew him, his call is still reverberating. Peter Brook's film, depicting his early life and its myth, may be thought of as an integral part of that call.

Pilgrim, Pilgrimage and Road was but Myself toward Myself.

'*Attār*

All things come into existence,
And thence we see them return,
Look at the things that have been flourishing:
Each goes back to its origin.

Tao Te Ching

On the angel's breast was the sign of the sacred
book of the Tarot—the square, and within
it the triangle. On his brow was the sign
of eternity and life—the circle.

Description of the Fourteenth Tarot Card

The ferryman punted them dexterously out from shore. Suddenly they saw a body in the
water, drifting rapidly down stream. Tripitaka stared at it in consternation. Monkey
laughed.

"Don't be frightened, Master," he said. "That's you."

And Pigsy said, "It's you, it's you."

Sandy clapped his hands. "It's you, it's you," he cried.

The ferryman too joined in the chorus. "There you *go!" he cried. "My best congratula-*
tions." He went on punting, and in a very short while they were all safe and sound at the
other side. Tripitaka stepped lightly ashore. He had discarded his earthly body; he was
cleansed from the corruption of the senses, from the fleshly inheritance of those bygone years.
His was now the transcendent wisdom that leads to the Further Shore, the mastery that knows
no bounds.

Wu Ch'èng-èn, Monkey

THE TEN
OXHERDING PICTURES

Kaku-an's Manual of Zen Training and Instruction

"The Bull"
I Anger, heart Dr. Schloegl explanation
Anger
Desire

Introduction

The meaning and spirit of this Oriental allegory, composed in the twelfth century as a training guide for Chinese Buddhist monks, has managed to survive many versions and interpretations. It is still used today as a teaching manual in Zen monasteries in Japan. But the experience of relating to a unifying element within oneself is not confined to Zen followers. Nor are the disciplinary approaches toward this experience, so vividly indicated by the different stages of training the ox, exclusively Zen.

People look for the Way in all directions—their search may bring them to the ends of the earth. But the Way, it is indicated, is not far. It is as near as oneself, as close as one's breath. The Way itself lies in wait for the seeker. The spell of Open Sesame, of finding the treasure that is right in front of one, repeats itself in all traditions. The seeker, however, must seek—and this is the core of his difficulty. For he cannot know what he is looking for until he finds it.

Like all authentic manuals of spiritual instruction, the oxherding theme is simple. But at the same time it is profound and subtle, pointing to the ultimate meaning of man's existence on earth.

Circle

What could be more simple than a man looking for his ox? But when we realize what the ox is, what could be more profound?

The Ten Oxherding Pictures reproduced here, and the poems and introductory words attached to them, are by Kaku-an Shi-en, a Zen master of the Sung dynasty. (Some sources attribute the Kaku-an pictures to the fifteenth-century sumiye *painter, Shubun.) There are earlier versions with five and eight pictures, ending with number eight, the empty circle. But Kaku-an realized that this was not the end of the story. It had to be shown, as now appears in number nine—Returning to the Source—that the ox from the beginning had never been missing. And further, that the ultimate stage of the search was neither the Void nor Nirvana, but the return of the enlightened seeker to the world of men.*

Kaku-an reached that stage of development where detachment and compassion, like eternity and time, are not incompatible. He does not keep his humanity distinct from his divinity. The quest is not merely to discover the treasure for oneself, but to share it with others, "to enter the city with bliss-bestowing hands."

To find out who you are, and to know that the ox is never missing, is not easy. Probably Kaku-an, kind-hearted Kaku-an, made these wonderful drawings because he knows how difficult it is to describe this experience in words. So he wills us these oxherding pictures and asks only that we look at them with an open heart.

Then . . . maybe, AHH!

William Segal

I   Searching for the Ox.

Searching for the Ox. The beast has never gone astray, and what is the use of searching for him? The reason why the oxherd is not on intimate terms with him is because the oxherd himself has violated his own inmost nature. The beast is lost, for the oxherd has himself been led out of the way through his deluding senses. His home is receding farther away from him, and byways and crossways are ever confused. Desire for gain and fear of loss burn like fire; ideas of right and wrong shoot up like a phalanx.

Alone in the wilderness, lost in the jungle, the boy is
    searching, searching!
The swelling waters, the far-away mountains, and
    the unending path;
Exhausted and in despair, he knows not where to go,
He only hears the evening cicadas singing in the
    maple-woods.

II Seeing the Traces.

Seeing the Traces. By the aid of the sutras and by inquiring into the doctrines, he has come to understand something, he has found the traces. He now knows that vessels, however varied, are all of one substance, and that the objective world is a reflection of the Self. Yet, he is unable to distinguish what is good from what is not, his mind is still confused as to truth and falsehood. As he has not yet entered the gate, he is provisionally said to have noticed the traces.

> By the stream and under the trees, scattered are the
>   traces of the lost;
> The sweet-scented grasses are growing thick—did he
>   find the way?
> However remote over the hills and far away the beast
>   may wander,
> His nose reaches the heavens and none can conceal it.

116

III Seeing the Ox.

Seeing the Ox. The boy finds the way by the sound he hears; he sees thereby into the origin of things, and all his senses are in harmonious order. In all his activities, it is manifestly present. It is like the salt in water and the glue in color. [It is there though not distinguishable as an individual entity.] When the eye is properly directed, he will find that it is no other than himself.

On a yonder branch perches a nightingale cheerfully
    singing;
The sun is warm, and a soothing breeze blows, on the
    bank the willows are green;
The ox is there all by himself, nowhere is he to hide
    himself;
The splendid head decorated with stately horns—
    what painter can reproduce him?

IV   Catching the Ox.

Catching the Ox. Long lost in the wilderness, the boy has at last found the ox and his hands are on him. But, owing to the overwhelming pressure of the outside world, the ox is hard to keep under control. He constantly longs for the old sweet-scented field. The wild nature is still unruly, and altogether refuses to be broken. If the oxherd wishes to see the ox completely in harmony with himself, he has surely to use the whip freely.

> With the energy of his whole being, the boy has at
>   last taken hold of the ox:
> But how wild his will, how ungovernable his power!
> At times he struts up a plateau,
> When lo! he is lost again in a misty impenetrable
>   mountain-pass.

V Herding the Ox.

Herding the Ox. When a thought moves, another follows, and then another—an endless train of thoughts is thus awakened. Through enlightenment all this turns into truth; but falsehood asserts itself when confusion prevails. Things oppress us not because of an objective world, but because of a self-deceiving mind. Do not let the nose-string loose, hold it tight, and allow no vacillation.

> The boy is not to separate himself with his whip and
>   tether,
> Lest the animal should wander away into a world of
>   defilements;
> When he is properly tended to, he will grow pure and
>   docile;
> Without a chain, nothing binding, he will by himself
>   follow the oxherd.

VI Coming Home on the Ox's Back.

Coming Home on the Ox's Back. The struggle is over; the man is no more concerned with gain and loss. He hums a rustic tune of the woodsman, he sings simple songs of the village boy. Saddling himself on the ox's back, his eyes are fixed on things not of the earth, earthy. Even if he is called, he will not turn his head; however enticed he will no more be kept back.

> Riding on the animal, he leisurely wends his way home:
> Enveloped in the evening mist, how tunefully the flute vanishes away!
> Singing a ditty, beating time, his heart is filled with a joy indescribable!
> That he is now one of those who know, need it be told?

VII   The Ox Forgotten, Leaving the Man Alone. (Begin*g of Serious religious train*g)

(The bull's fully humanized)

The Ox Forgotten, Leaving the Man Alone. The dharmas are one and the ox is symbolic. When you know that what you need is not the snare or set-net but the hare or fish, it is like gold separated from the dross, it is like the moon rising out of the clouds. The one ray of light serene and penetrating shines even before days of creation.

> Riding on the animal, he is at last back in his home,
> Where lo! the ox is no more; the man alone sits
>   serenely.
> Though the red sun is high up in the sky, he is still
>   quietly dreaming,
> Under a straw-thatched roof are his whip and rope
>   idly lying.

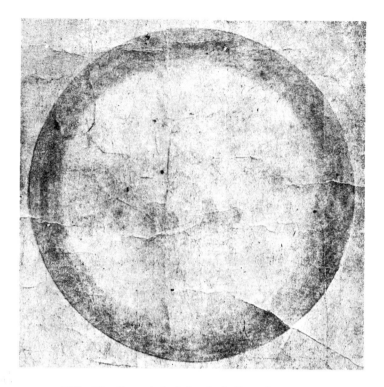

VIII   *The Ox and the Man Both Gone Out of Sight.*

The Ox and the Man Both Gone out of Sight. All confusion is set aside, and serenity alone prevails; even the idea of holiness does not obtain. He does not linger about where the Buddha is, and as to where there is no Buddha he speedily passes by. When there exists no form of dualism, even a thousand-eyed one fails to detect a loop-hole. A holiness before which birds offer flowers is but a farce.

All is empty—the whip, the rope, the man, and the
ox:
Who can ever survey the vastness of heaven?
Over the furnace burning ablaze, not a flake of snow
can fall:
When this state of things obtains, manifest is the spirit
of the ancient master.

IX   Returning to the Origin, Back to the Source.

Returning to the Origin, Back to the Source. From the very beginning, pure and immaculate, the man has never been affected by defilement. He watches the growth and decay of things, while himself abiding in the immovable serenity of nonassertion. He does not identify himself with the maya-like transformations that are going on about him. The waters are blue, the mountains are green; sitting alone, he observes things undergoing changes.

> To return to the Origin, to be back at the Source—
>   already a false step this!
> Far better it is to stay at home, blind and deaf, and
>   without much ado;
> Sitting in the hut, he takes no cognizance of things
>   outside,
> Behold the streams flowing—whither nobody knows;
>   and the flowers vividly red—for whom are they?

X Entering the City with Bliss-bestowing Hands.

Entering the City with Bliss-bestowing Hands. His thatched cottage gate is closed, and even the wisest know him not. No glimpses of his inner life are to be caught; for he goes on his own way without following the steps of the ancient sages. Carrying a gourd he goes out into the market, leaning against a staff he comes home. He is found in company with wine-bibbers and butchers; he and they are all converted into Buddhas.

Bare-chested and bare-footed, he comes out into the
  market-place;
Daubed with mud and ashes, how broadly he smiles!
There is no need for the miraculous power of the gods,
For he touches, and lo! the dead trees are in full
  bloom.

THE CONFERENCE OF THE BIRDS

Farīd ud-Dīn 'Attār's Parable of the Quest

Introduction

From Biblical times the symbol of the bird in flight, soaring in another dimension, liberated from the forces binding man to earth, has been central in the poetic and mystical literature of the Near East. While the Ark was still on the flood, after the mountain tops appeared, the raven was sent out and "went to and fro." In an unknown world the only reality was its own image, reflected in the cosmic waters. Without that prior dark symbol the mission of the dove would be less significant, for the olive leaf offered in its silent beak denotes survival rather than search.

As a way of life was reestablished among the valleys, deserts and mountain ranges, the search went on. Again the raven appeared, to sustain Elijah in the Jordan valley; later still the dove was seen again, silent but accompanied by symbolic words; and the Essene voice, "the voice of one crying in the wilderness," was heard. That cry echoed from the Jordan to the Nile, from the deserts of Egypt to those of **Arabia deserta**; *from the Hijāz to the Euphrates valley, a return to its antediluvian source.*

In Baghdad, in that valley, three centuries before 'Attār, al-Hallāj had sung in ecstasy:

I am He whom I love, and He whom I love is I;
We are two spirits dwelling in one body.
If thou seest me, thou seest Him,
And if thou seest Him, thou seest us both.

125

Circle

For his words he was tried, tortured and crucified. The burning spirit of al-Hallāj, after the long slow growth and blossoming of mystical poetry in Khorasan, had inspired 'Attār; shortly before his time, Sanā'ī had written a qasīda, *"The Litany of the Birds," in which each bird praises God in his own special way. Did Sanā'ī's idea inspire 'Attār? We do not know.*

The poverty of our knowledge of many of the great Persian poets and mystics enwraps them as the patched and worn khirka *of the Sūfī does its owner. These men, living lives of piety and asceticism, fasting and prayer, sought anonymity. Even the dates of 'Attār's life cannot be fixed with certainty. It is known that he was a pharmacist by trade, that he lived in Khorasan in the latter part of the twelfth century and well on into the thirteenth, and that he wrote much.* The Conference of the Birds *is his most famous work.*

This very lack of data reveals the vision giving rise to such literature —the world itself being but the shadow of its divine cause. In 'Attār's own words:

> *If the Simurgh had not wished to manifest himself he would not have cast his shadow; if he had wished to remain hidden his shadow would not have appeared in the world.*

The Conference of the Birds *is the story of the search for the Simurgh, the King of the birds, under the leadership of the Hoopoe; since she had been the confidant of Solomon and had received her crown from him, all the birds of the world assembled and listened to her as she spoke:*

> *Do not imagine that the journey is short; one must have the heart of a lion to follow this unusual road, for it is very long and the sea is deep. . . . A man must not keep his soul from the beloved, but must be in a fitting state to lead his soul to the court of the King.*

Many of the birds present began to make their excuses; finally the resolute ones set out together.

Their way lay through seven valleys: that of the Quest, then that of Love, that of Understanding, that of Detachment, that of Unity, that of

Bewilderment, and lastly that of Death. In the description of them the contrast of the sunlight and shadow of reality is stark:

> *When you enter the first valley, the Valley of the Quest, a hundred difficulties will assail you, you will undergo a hundred trials. . . . You will have to spend several years there, you will have to make great efforts and to change your state.*

'Attar softens this relief for the reader with many poetic allegories, digressions, tales and parables, which convey a sense of timeless life within the trivial, enhance a dimension of spirit within the flight of the soul searching for the truth. In the rendering given here some of these passages are omitted and at times the concentration of light is hard to bear, as it was for the company of birds themselves:

> *In the end, only a small number of all this great company arrived at that sublime place to which the Hoopoe had led them. Of the thousands of birds almost all had disappeared. . . . Many, who had started out from curiosity or pleasure, perished without an idea of what they had set out to find.*

At last, having left behind them the Valley of Death, the thirty birds who are still together arrive at the end of their journey. At the palace of the Simurgh they are received by a noble chamberlain who, having first tested them, opens the door and then:

> *As he drew aside a hundred curtains, one after the other, a new world beyond the veil was revealed.*

Christopher Fremantle

Drawings by Rosemary Nott

Circle

The Conference Opens

All the birds of the world, known and unknown, were assembled together. They said: "No country in the world is without a king. How comes it, then, that the kingdom of the birds is without a ruler! This state of things cannot last. We must make effort together and search for one; for no country can have a good administration and a good organization without a king."

So they began to consider how to set out on their quest. The Hoopoe, excited and full of hope, came forward and placed herself in the middle of the assembled birds. On her breast was the ornament which symbolized that she had entered the way of spiritual knowledge; the crest on her head was as the crown of truth, and she had knowledge of both good and evil.

"Dear Birds," she began, "I am one who is engaged in divine warfare, and I am a messenger of the world invisible. I have knowledge of God and of the secrets of creation. When one carries on his beak, as I do, the name of God, Bismillah, it follows that one must have knowledge of many hidden things. Yet my days pass restlessly and I am concerned with no person for I am wholly occupied by love for the King. For years I have traveled by sea and land, over mountains and valleys. I covered an immense space in the time of the deluge; I accompanied Solomon on his journeys, and I have measured the bounds of the world.

"I know well my King, but alone I cannot set out to find him. Abandon your timidity, your self-conceit and your unbelief, for he who makes light of his own life is delivered from himself; he is delivered from good and evil in the way of his Beloved. Be generous with your life. Set your feet upon the earth and step out joyfully for the court of the King. We have a true King, he lives behind the mountains called Kāf. His name is Simurgh and he is the King of birds. He is close to us, but we are far from him. The place where he dwells is inaccessible, and no tongue is able to utter his name. Before him hang a hundred thousand veils of light and darkness, and in the two worlds no one has power to dispute his kingdom. He is the sovereign Lord and is bathed in the perfection of his majesty. He does not manifest himself completely even in the place of his dwelling, and to this no knowledge or intelligence can

attain. The way is unknown, and no one has the steadfastness to seek it, though thousands of creatures spend their lives in longing. Even the purest soul cannot describe him, neither can the reason comprehend: these two eyes are blind. The wise cannot discover his perfection nor can the man of understanding perceive his beauty. All creatures have wished to attain to this perfection and beauty by imagination. But how can you tread that path with thought? How measure the moon from the fish? So, thousands of heads go here and there, like the ball in polo, and only lamentations and sighs of longing are heard. Many lands and seas are on the way. Do not imagine that the journey is short; one must have the heart of a lion to follow this unusual road, for it is very long and the sea is deep. One plods along in a state of amazement, sometimes smiling, sometimes weeping. As for me, I shall be happy to discover even a trace of him. . . . A man must not keep his soul from the beloved, but must be in a fitting state to lead his soul to the court of the King.

"An astonishing thing! The first manifestation of the Simurgh took place in China in the middle of the night. One of his feathers fell on China and his reputation filled the world. Everyone made a picture of this feather, and from it formed his own system of ideas, and so fell into a turmoil. This feather is still in the picture-gallery of that country; hence the saying, 'Seek knowledge, even in China!'

"But for his manifestation there would not have been so much noise in the world concerning this mysterious Being. This sign of his existence is a token of his glory. All souls carry an impression of the image of his feather. Since the description of it has neither head nor tail, beginning nor end, it is not necessary to say more about it. Now, any of you who are for this road, prepare yourselves, and put your feet on the Way."

When the Hoopoe had finished the birds began excitedly to discuss the glory of this King, and seized with longing to have him for their own sovereign they were all impatient to be off. They resolved to go together; each became a friend to the other and an enemy to himself. But when they began to realize how long and painful their journey was to be, they hesitated, and in spite of their apparent goodwill began to excuse themselves, each according to his type.

The Conference of the Birds

The Nightingale

The amorous Nightingale first came forward, almost beside himself with passion. He poured emotion into each of the thousand notes of his song; and in each was to be found a world of secrets. When he sang of these mysteries the birds became silent. "The secrets of love are known to me," he said. "All night I repeat my songs of love. Is there no unhappy David to whom I can sing the yearning psalms of love? The flute's sweet wailing is because of me, and the lamenting of the lute. When love overpowers my soul my singing is as the sighing sea. So deep in love am I with the Rose that I do not even think of my own existence, but only of the Rose and the coral of her petals. The journey to the Simurgh is beyond my strength; the love of the Rose is enough for the Nightingale. It is for me that she flowers with her hundred petals; what more, then, can I wish!"

The Hoopoe replied: "O Nightingale, you who would stay behind dazzled by the exterior form of things, cease to delight in an attachment so deluding. The love of the Rose has many thorns; it has disturbed and dominated you. Although the Rose is fair, her beauty is soon gone. One who seeks self-perfection should not become the slave of a love so passing. Forsake the Rose and blush for yourself: for she laughs at you with each new Spring and then she smiles no more."

The Peacock

Next came the golden Peacock, with feathers of a hundred—what shall I say?—a hundred thousand colors! He displayed himself, turning this way and that, like a bride. "The painter of the world," he said, "to fashion me took in his hand the brush of the jinn. But although I am Gabriel among birds my lot is not to be envied. I was friendly with the serpent in the earthly paradise, and for this was ignominiously driven out. They deprived me of a position of trust, they, who trusted me, and my feet were my prison. But I am always hoping that some benevolent guide will lead me out of this dark abode and take me to the everlasting mansions. I do not expect to reach the King you speak of, it will suffice

131

me to reach his gate. How can you expect me to strive to reach the Simurgh since I have lived in the earthly paradise? I have no wish except to dwell there again. Nothing else has any meaning for me."

The Hoopoe replied: "You are straying from the true Way. The palace of this King is far better than your paradise. You cannot do better than to strive to reach it. It is the habitation of the soul, it is eternity, it is the object of our real desires, the dwelling of the heart, the seat of truth. The Most High is a vast ocean; the paradise of earthly bliss is only a little drop; all that is not this ocean is distraction. When you can have the ocean why will you seek a drop of evening dew? Shall he who shares the secrets of the sun idle with a speck of dust? Is he who has all, concerned with the part? Is the soul concerned with members of the body? If you would be perfect, seek the whole, choose the whole, be whole."

The Sparrow

Then came the Sparrow, of feeble body and tender heart, trembling like a flame from head to foot. She said: "I am dumbfounded and crestfallen. I don't know how to exist, and I am frail as a hair. I have no one to help me and I have not the strength of an ant. I have neither down nor feathers—nothing. How can a weakling like me make her way to the Simurgh? A sparrow could never do it. There is no lack of those in the world who seek this union, but for a being such as I it is not becoming. I do not wish to begin such a toilsome journey for something I can never reach. If I should start out for the court of the Simurgh I should be consumed on the way. So, since I am not at all fitted for this enterprise, I shall be content to seek here my Joseph in the well. If I find him and draw him out, I shall soar with him from the fish to the moon."

The Hoopoe replied: "O you, who in your despondency are sometimes sad, sometimes gay, I am not deceived by these artful pleas. You are a little hypocrite. Even in your humility you show a hundred signs of vanity and pride. Not another word, sew up your lips and put your foot forward. If you burn, you will burn with the others. And don't compare yourself with Joseph!"

The Peacock

Circle

Discussion Between the Hoopoe and the Birds

Then all the birds, one after another, began to make foolish excuses. If I do not repeat them, pardon me, reader, for it would take too long. But how can such birds hope to entangle the Simurgh in their claws? So the Hoopoe continued her discourse:

"He who prefers the Simurgh to his own life must struggle bravely with himself. If your gizzard will not digest a single grain, how shall you share in the feasting of the Simurgh? When you hesitate over a sip of wine, how will you drink a large cup, O paladin? If you have not the energy for an atom, how shall you find the treasure of the sun? If you can drown in a drop of water, how will you go from the depths of the sea to the heavenly heights? This is not a simple perfume; and neither is it a task for him who has not a clean face."

When the birds had thought this over they again spoke to the Hoopoe: "You have taken upon yourself the task of showing us the way, you, the best and most powerful of birds. But we are feeble, with neither down nor feathers, so how shall we be able at last to reach the sublime Simurgh? If we should arrive it would be a miracle. Tell us something about this marvelous Being by means of a similitude, or, blind as we are, we shall understand nothing of the mystery. If there were some relation between this Being and ourselves it would be much easier for us to set out. But, as we see it, he may be compared to Solomon, and we to begging ants. How can an insect in the bottom of a pit mount up to the great Simurgh? Shall royalty be the portion of the beggar?"

Reply of the Hoopoe

The Hoopoe said: "O birds without aspiration! How shall love spring bountifully in a heart devoid of sensibility? Begging the question like this, which seems to gratify you, will result in nothing. He who loves sets out with open eyes toward his goal, making a plaything of his life.

"When the Simurgh manifested himself outside the veil, radiant as the sun, he produced thousands of shadows on earth. When he cast his

134

glance on these shadows, there appeared birds in great numbers. The diffent types of birds that are seen in the world are thus only the shadow of the Simurgh. Know then, O ignorant ones, that when you understand this you will understand exactly your relation to the Simurgh. Ponder over this mystery, but do not reveal it. He who acquires this knowledge sinks into the immensity of the Simurgh; though he must not think that he is God on that account.

"If you become this of which I speak you will not be God, but you will be immersed in God. Does a man thus immersed become transubstantiated? When you understand of whom you are the shadow you will become indifferent to life or death. If the Simurgh had not wished to manifest himself he would not have cast his shadow; if he had wished to remain hidden his shadow would not have appeared in the world. All that which is produced by his shadow becomes visible. If your spirit is not fit to see the Simurgh, neither will your heart be a bright mirror fit to reflect him. It is true that no eye is able to contemplate and marvel at his beauty, nor is it capable of understanding; one cannot feel toward the Simurgh as one feels toward the beauty of this world. But by his abounding grace he has given us a mirror to reflect himself, and this mirror is the heart. Look into your heart and there you will see his image."

When she had finished her discourse the birds began to understand something of the ancient mysteries, and the relation between themselves and the Simurgh. The thought of the Simurgh lifted them out of their apathy; love for him alone filled their hearts, and they began to consider how to start on the journey.

The Birds Set Out

At the setting-out place, so great was the number of birds who flocked there that they hid the moon and the fish; but when they saw the entrance to the first valley, they flew up to the clouds in fright. Then, with much fluttering of wings and feathers and mutual encouragement, their eagerness to renounce everything revived. But the task before them was heavy and the way was long. Silence brooded over the road which stretched before them and a bird asked the Hoopoe why it was

so deserted. "Because of the awe that the King inspires, to whose dwelling it leads," she answered.

Fear and apprehension drew plaintive cries from the birds as they faced a road without end, where the strong wind of detachment from earthly things split the vault of heaven. In their anxiety they crowded together and asked the Hoopoe for advice. They said, "We do not know how we should present ourselves to the King with due reverence. But you have been in the presence of Solomon, and know the usages of etiquette. Also you have ascended and descended this road, and many times flown round the earth. You are our Imām, to bind and to loose. We ask you now to go up into the minabar and instruct us. Tell us about the road and about the King's court and the ceremonies there, for we do not wish to behave foolishly. Also, all kinds of difficulties arise in our minds, and for this journey one needs to be free from disquiet."

The Description of the First Valley
or
The Valley of the Quest

The Hoopoe replied: "We have seven valleys to cross and only after we have crossed them shall we discover the Simurgh. No one has ever come back into the world who has made this journey, and it is impossible to say how many parasangs there are in front of us. Be patient, O fearful ones, since all those who went by this road were in your state.

"When you enter the first valley, the Valley of the Quest, a hundred difficulties will assail you; you will undergo a hundred trials. There, the parrot of heaven is no more than a fly. You will have to spend several years there, you will have to make great efforts, and to change your state. You will have to give up all that has seemed precious to you and regard as nothing all that you possess. When you are sure that you possess nothing, you will still have to detach yourself from all that exists. Your heart will then be saved from perdition and you will see the pure light of Divine Majesty and your real wishes will be multiplied to infinity. One who enters here will be filled with such longing that he will give himself up completely to the quest."

Circle

The Second Valley
or
The Valley of Love

The Hoopoe continued: "The next valley is the Valley of Love. To enter it one must be a flaming fire—what shall I say? A man must himself be fire.

"In this valley, love is represented by fire, and reason by smoke. When love comes, reason disappears. Reason cannot live with the folly of love; love has nothing to do with human reason. If you possessed inner sight, the atoms of the visible world would be manifested to you. But if you look at things with the eye of ordinary reason you will never understand how necessary it is to love. Only a man who has been tested and is free can feel this. He who undertakes this journey should have a thousand hearts so that he can sacrifice one at every moment."

The Third Valley
or
The Valley of Understanding

The Hoopoe continued: "After the valley of which I have spoken, there comes another—the Valley of Understanding, which has neither beginning nor end. No way is equal to this way, and the distance to be traveled to cross it is beyond reckoning.

"Understanding, for each traveler, is enduring; but knowledge is temporary. The soul, like the body, is in a state of progress or decline; and the Spiritual Way reveals itself only in the degree to which the traveler has overcome his faults and weaknesses, his sleep and his inertia, and each will approach nearer to his aim according to his effort. When the sun of understanding brightens this road, each receives light according to his merit and he finds the degree assigned to him in the understanding of truth.

"But how many have lost their way in this search, for one who has found the mysteries! It is necessary to have a deep and lasting wish to become as we ought to be in order to cross this difficult valley.

"As for you who are asleep (and I cannot commend you for this), why not put on mourning? You who have not seen the beauty of your

138

friend, get up and search! How long will you stay as you are, like a donkey without a halter!"

The Fourth Valley

or

The Valley of

Independence and Detachment

The Hoopoe continued: "Then comes the valley where there is neither the desire to possess nor the wish to discover. In this state of the soul a cold wind blows, so violent that in a moment it devastates an immense space; the seven oceans are no .more than a pool, the seven planets a mere spark, the seven heavens a corpse, the seven hells broken ice. Then, an astonishing thing, beyond reason! An ant has the strength of a hundred elephants, and a hundred caravans perish while a rook is filling his crop.

"In this valley nothing old or new has value; you can act or not act. If you saw a whole world burning until hearts were only shish kebab, it would be only a dream compared to reality. If myriads of souls were to fall into this boundless ocean it would be as a drop of dew. If heaven and earth were to burst into minute particles it would be no more than a leaf falling from a tree; and if everything were to be annihilated, from the fish to the moon, would there be found in the depths of a pit the leg of a lame ant? If there remain no trace of either men or jinn, the secret of a drop of water from which all has been formed is still to be pondered over."

The Fifth Valley

or

The Valley of Unity

The Hoopoe continued: "You will next have to cross the Valley of Unity. In this valley everything is broken in pieces and then unified. All who raise their heads here raise them from the same collar. Although you seem to see many beings, in reality there is only one—all make one

139

which is complete in its unity. Again, that which you see as a unity is not different from that which appears as number. And as the Being of whom I speak is beyond unity and numbering, cease to think of eternity as before and after, and since these two eternities have vanished, cease to speak of them. When all that is visible is reduced to nothing, what is there left to contemplate?"

The Sixth Valley
or
The Valley of Astonishment
and Bewilderment

After the Valley of Unity comes the Valley of Astonishment and Bewilderment, where one is a prey to sadness and dejection. There sighs are like swords, and each breath a bitter sigh; there is sorrow and lamentation, and a burning eagerness. It is at once day and night. There is fire, yet a man is depressed and despondent. How, in his bewilderment, shall he continue his way? But he who has achieved unity forgets all and forgets himself. If he is asked: "Are you, or are you not? Have you or have you not the feeling of existence? Are you in the middle or on the border? Are you mortal or immortal?" he will reply with certainty: "I know nothing, I understand nothing, I am unaware of myself. I am in love, but with whom I do not know. My heart is at the same time both full and empty of love."

The Seventh Valley
or
The Valley of Deprivation and Death

The Hoopoe continued: "Last of all comes the Valley of Deprivation and Death, which it is almost impossible to describe. The essence of this valley is forgetfulness, dumbness, deafness and distraction; the thousand shadows which surround you disappear in a single ray of the celestial sun. When the ocean of immensity begins to heave, the pattern on its surface loses its form; and this pattern is no other than the world present and the world to come. Whoever declares that he does not exist acquires great merit. The drop that becomes part of this great ocean abides there for ever and in peace. In this calm sea, a man, at first, experiences only humiliation and overthrow; but when he emerges from this state he will understand it as creation, and many secrets will be revealed to him."

Attitude of the Birds

When the birds had listened to this discourse of the Hoopoe their heads drooped down, and sorrow pierced their hearts. Now they understood how difficult it would be for a handful of dust like themselves to bend such a bow. So great was their agitation that numbers of them died then and there. But others, in spite of their distress, decided to set out on the long road. For years they traveled over mountains and valleys, and a great part of their life flowed past on this journey. But how is it possible to relate all that happened to them? It would be necessary to go with them and see their difficulties for oneself, and to follow the wanderings of this long road. Only then could one realize what the birds suffered.

In the end, only a small number of all this great company arrived at that sublime place to which the Hoopoe had led them. Of the thousands of birds almost all had disappeared. Many had been lost in the ocean, others had perished on the summits of the high mountains, tortured by thirst; others had had their wings burnt and their hearts dried up by the fire of the sun; others were devoured by tigers and panthers; others died of fatigue in the deserts and in the wilderness, their lips parched and their bodies overcome by the heat; some went mad and killed each other for a grain of barley; others, enfeebled by suffering and weariness, dropped on the road unable to go further; others, bewildered by the things they saw, stopped where they were, stupefied; and many, who had started out from curiosity or pleasure, perished without an idea of what they had set out to find.

So then, out of all those thousands of birds, only thirty reached the end of the journey. And even these were bewildered, weary and dejected, with neither feathers nor wings. But now they were at the door of this Majesty that cannot be described, whose essence is incomprehensible—that Being who is beyond human reason and knowledge.

Then flashed the lightning of fulfillment, and a hundred worlds were consumed in a moment. They saw thousands of suns each more resplendent than the other, thousands of moons and stars all equally beautiful, and seeing all this they were amazed and agitated like a dancing atom of dust, and they cried out: "O Thou who art more radiant than the sun! Thou, who hast reduced the sun to an atom, how can we appear before Thee? Ah, why have we so uselessly endured all this suffering on the Way? Having renounced ourselves and all things, we now cannot obtain that for which we have striven. Here, it little matters whether we exist or not."

Then the birds, who were so disheartened that they resembled a cock half-killed, sank into despair. A long time passed. When, at a propitious moment, the door suddenly opened, there stepped out a noble chamberlain, one of the courtiers of the Supreme Majesty. He looked them over and saw that out of thousands only these thirty birds were left.

He said: "Now then, O Birds, where have you come from, and what are you doing here? What is your name? O you who are destitute of everything, where is your home? What do they call you in the world? What can be done with a feeble handful of dust like you?"

"We have come," they said, "to acknowledge the Simurgh as our King. Through love and desire for him we have lost our reason and our peace of mind. Very long ago, when we started on this journey, we were thousands, and now only thirty of us have arrived at this sublime court. We cannot believe that the King will scorn us after all the sufferings we have gone through. Ah, no! He cannot but look on us with the eye of benevolence!"

The Chamberlain replied: "O you whose minds and hearts are troubled, whether you exist or do not exist in the universe, the King has his being always and eternally. Thousands of worlds of creatures are no more than an ant at his gate. You bring nothing but moans and lamentations. Return then to whence you came, O vile handful of earth!"

At this, the birds were petrified with astonishment. Nevertheless, when they came to themselves a little, they said: "Will this great King reject us so ignominiously? And if he really has this attitude to us may he not change it to one of honor? Remember Majnūn who said, 'If all the people who dwell on earth wished to sing my praises, I would not accept them; I would rather have the insults of Laīla. One of her insults is more to me than a hundred compliments from another woman.' "

"The lightning of his glory manifests itself," said the Chamberlain, "and it lifts up the reason of all souls. What benefit is there if the soul be consumed by a hundred sorrows? What benefit is there at this moment in either greatness or littleness?"

The birds, on fire with love, said: "How can the moth save itself from the flame when it wishes to be one with the flame? The friend we seek will content us by allowing us to be united to him. If now we are refused, what is there left for us to do? We are like the moth who wished for union with the flame of the candle. They begged him not to sacrifice himself so foolishly and for such an impossible aim, but he thanked them for their advice and told them that since his heart was given to the flame forever, nothing else mattered."

Then the Chamberlain, having tested them, opened the door; and as he drew aside a hundred curtains, one after the other, a new world beyond the veil was revealed. Now was the Light of lights manifested, and all of them sat down on the masnad, the seat of the Majesty and Glory. They were given a writing which they were told to read through; and reading this, and pondering, they were able to understand their state. When they were completely at peace and detached from all things they became aware that the Simurgh was there with them, and a new life began for them in the Simurgh. All that they had done previously was washed away. The sun of majesty sent forth his rays, and in the reflection of each other's faces these thirty birds (si-murgh) of the outer world contemplated the face of the Simurgh of the inner world. This so astonished them that they did not know if they were still themselves or if they had become the Simurgh. At last, in a state of contemplation, they realized that they were the Simurgh and that the Simurgh was the thirty birds. When they gazed at the Simurgh they saw that it was truly the Simurgh who was there, and when they turned their eyes toward themselves they saw that they themselves were the Simurgh. And perceiving both at once, themselves and Him, they realized that they and the Simurgh were one and the same being. No one in the world has ever heard of anything to equal it.

Then they gave themselves up to meditation, and after a little they asked the Simurgh, without the use of tongues, to reveal to them the secret of the mystery of the unity and plurality of beings. The Simurgh, also without speaking, made this reply: "The sun of my majesty is a mirror. He who sees himself therein sees his soul and his body, and sees them completely. Since you have come as thirty birds, si-murgh, you will see thirty birds in this mirror. If forty or fifty were to come, it would be the same. Although you are now completely changed you see yourselves as you were before.

"Can the sight of an ant reach to the far-off Pleiades? And can this insect lift an anvil? Have you ever seen a gnat seize an elephant in its teeth? All that you have known, all that you have seen, all that you have said or heard—all this is no longer that. When you crossed the valleys of the Spiritual Way and when you performed good tasks, you did all this by my action; and you were able to see the valleys of my essence and my perfections. You, who are only thirty birds, did well to be astonished, impatient and wondering. But I am more than thirty birds. I am the very essence of the true Simurgh. Annihilate then yourselves gloriously and joyfully in me, and in me you shall find yourselves."

Thereupon, the birds at last lost themselves for ever in the Simurgh —the shadow was lost in the sun, and that is all.

Contributors

EDWIN BERNBAUM spent two years in the Peace Corps in Nepal and India. His forthcoming book is on the Tibetan myth of Shambhala.

JOSEPH CARY teaches at the University of Connecticut. He is the author of a book on modern Italian poetry.

D. M. DOOLING is editor and publisher of *Parabola: the Magazine of Myth and Tradition.*

CHRISTOPHER FREMANTLE was a peripatetic painter, editor and translator. He died when this book was in press.

JAMES GEORGE has been Canadian Ambassador to India, Iran, Sri Lanka, Nepal and Kuwait. He is now director of the Threshold Foundation.

PAUL JORDAN-SMITH is a storyteller and an Associate Editor of *Parabola.*

ROGER LIPSEY, author and editor of the Ananda K. Coomaraswamy trilogy (Bollingen Series, Princeton University Press, 1977), has taught the history of art and traditional literature in several American universities.

PETER MATTHIESSEN is the world-traveling author of eight books on exploration and natural history *(Wildlife in America; The Tree Where Man was Born; The Snow Leopard)* and five novels *(At Play in the Fields of the Lord; Far Tortuga).*

JACOB NEEDLEMAN is Professor of Philosophy at San Francisco State University. He is author of *The New Religions* and *A Sense of the Cosmos,* and editor of several anthologies.

WILLIAM SEGAL is the publisher of *American Fabrics* magazine. He has made frequent visits to Zen monasteries in Japan.

P. L. TRAVERS, author of the Mary Poppins books, *Friend Monkey, The Fox at the Manger,* and lecturer on myth, legend and fairy tale, was a writer-in-residence at Radcliffe, Smith and Claremont before she returned to London. Her most recent book is *Two Pairs of Shoes.*

Text Credits

1. *Two Tales by Martin Buber.* "The Treasure" and "A Vain Search." Reprinted by permission of Schocken Books, Inc., from *Tales of the Hasidim: The Later Masters,* by Martin Buber, Schocken Books, Inc., 1948; copyright renewed 1975.

2. *Gilgamesh: The Search for Eternal Life.* Page 50: Ten lines of free verse from G. I. Gurdjieff, *Meetings with Remarkable Men,* E. P. Dutton & Co., 1963. Courtesy of E. P. Dutton & Co. and Triangle Editions, Inc. Page 53: Eleven lines of free verse from "Gilgamesh," by Nigel Dennis, reprinted by permission of *Horizon,* Summer 1973. © 1973 by American Heritage Publishing Co., Inc.

3. *A Dialogue Between One and Zero.* Used with the kind permission of the Reverend Sōhaku Kobori. Reprinted from *The Eastern Buddhist,* Old Series, VIII: 3 (November 1957).

4. *The Hymn of the Pearl.* Adapted from Hans Jonas, *The Gnostic Religion,* pp. 113–116, Beacon Press, © 1958 by Hans Jonas. Used with permission of Beacon Press and Hans Jonas. Other translations consulted: "The Hymn of the Soul" in M. R. James, *The Apocryphal New Testament,* Oxford, Clarendon Press, 1926; W. Wright, *Apocryphal Acts of the Apostles,* edited from Syriac manuscripts in the British Museum and other libraries, Williams and Norgate: London and Edinburgh, Vol. 1, 1871; "The Hymn of the Soul" in A. A. Bevan, *Texts and Studies, Contributions to Biblical and Patristic Literature,* Vol. 5, No. 3, edited by J. A. Robinson, Cambridge, 1897.

5. *The Ten Oxherding Pictures.* Kaku-an's text accompanying the pictures, translated into English by D. T. Suzuki, from D. T. Suzuki, *The Manual of Zen Buddhism,* Rider & Co., 1956; Grove Press, 1960. Used with the permission of Shokin Furuta, the Matsugaoka Bunko Foundation, Kamakura.

6. *The Conference of the Birds.* An abridgement of Farīd ud-Dīn 'Attār, *The Conference of the Birds,* rendered into English from the French translation of Garcin de Tassy by C. S. Nott, Janus Press, 1954; Routledge & Kegan Paul Ltd., 1961. Abridgement approved by C. S. Nott and used with the kind permission of Routledge & Kegan Paul.

Art Notes
and Picture Credits

Cover: "Le Grand Livre." Color drawing in mixed media, 1969, by Roland Topor. Collection of Mrs. Christopher Burge. Courtesy, Lefebre Gallery. Photograph: David Allison.

Frontispiece: Hakuin Ekaku, "The Bridge of Mama," seventeenth-century ink drawing. Courtesy, Harcourt Brace Jovanovich, Inc. First published in Isshū Miura and Ruth Fuller Sasaki, *The Zen Koan,* Harcourt Brace Jovanovich, Inc., 1965. Photograph: David Allison.

Introduction: "Circle, Triangle and Square." Ink drawing by Gibbon Sengai (1750–1837). Courtesy, Idemitsu Art Gallery, Tokyo.

Square

Page 1: Detail from Sengai's "Circle, Triangle and Square." Courtesy, Idemitsu Art Gallery, Tokyo.

Page 9: UNICEF poster by Ilonka Karasz. Photograph: David Allison.

Page 16: Late nineteenth-century Tibetan *thanka.* Courtesy, Musée Guimet, Paris. Photograph: Musées Nationaux, Paris.

Page 17: Pen drawing by Tenzin Namdak. Courtesy, David L. Snellgrove. From David L. Snellgrove, *The Nine Ways of Bon,* Oxford University Press, 1967.

Page 20: Section of a Chinese handscroll, "Dreaming of Immortality in a Thatched Cottage," ink and color on paper, attributed to Chou Ch'en, early sixteenth century. Courtesy, the Smithsonian Institution, Freer Gallery of Art, Washington, D.C.

Page 36: "Shadow Prisoner," first published in Arthur Tress, *Shadow*, Avon Books, 1975. Courtesy, Arthur Tress.

Page 45 and page 47: Paintings by Dino Cavallari, created for Herbert Mason, author of *Gilgamesh, A Verse Narrative*, Houghton Mifflin Company, Boston, 1971. Photographs: David Allison.

Triangle

Page 55: Detail from Sengai's "Circle, Triangle and Square." Courtesy, Idemitsu Art Gallery, Tokyo.

Page 60: Leaf F , from an Album of Landscapes by Tao-chi, 1641–ca. 1710. Courtesy, The Arthur M. Sackler Collection, The Art Museum, Princeton University.

Page 61: Early fourteenth-century French manuscript (MS 806), The Pierpont Morgan Library, New York.

Page 64: *Viraf-nameh*, an Indian manuscript (MS Indien 721), Bibliothèque Nationale, Paris.

Page 69: Mu-ch'i (Mokkei), thirteenth century, Chinese. Ryōkōin Collection, Daitokuji Temple, Kyoto; kindness of Professor Ernest Sato, University of Kyoto, and Fumiaki Hashimoto.

Page 79: "Draco," from *The Book of the Fixed Stars*, by 'Abdal-Rahmān b. 'Umar al-Sūfī, MS Marsh. 144, p. 54. Courtesy, the Curators of the Bodleian Library, Oxford.

Page 83: Seventeenth-century Serbian copy of a Byzantine manuscript, the Cosmos Indicopleustes. From Vojislav Mole, *Minijature iz g. 1649 sa Sestodneva Kozme Indikoplōva*, Srpska Kraljevska Akademija, XLIV, 1922, pl. XXIV. Courtesy, Oriental Division, The New York Public Library,

Art Notes and Picture Credits

Astor, Lenox and Tilden Foundations. Kindness of Jill Cowan and Zoran Tosic.

Page 86: Twelfth-century Hermetic manuscript(MS Lat. 3236A), Bibliothèque Nationale, Paris. Photograph: Bibliothèque Nationale.

Page 89: Thirteenth-century Armenian manuscript (MS 365), Library of St. Thoros. Courtesy, Armenian Patriarchate Manuscript Library, Jerusalem. Photograph: Garo Nalbandian.

Page 91: "Lao-Tzu." Color on silk, by Yokoyama Taikan, 1868–1958. Courtesy, Takashi Yokoyama.

Page 98: Ceramic design by Bernard Leach. Courtesy, *Cent Idées,* Paris. Photograph: Jean-Denis Mahn.

Page 103: Still from the film, "Meetings with Remarkable Men." Courtesy, Remar Productions, Inc.

Circle

Page 111: Detail from Sengai's "Circle, Triangle and Square." Courtesy, Idemitsu Art Gallery, Tokyo.

Page 115ff: Ten round paintings mounted in one handscroll, fifteenth century, traditionally attributed to Shūbun, Shōkokuji Temple, Kyoto. Courtesy, the Matsugaoka Bunko Foundation, Kamakura.

Page 129ff: Line drawings by Rosemary Nott.